NETSCAPE *Composer*

CREATING WEB PAGES

Gary B. Shelly
Thomas J. Cashman
John F. Repede

SHELLY
CASHMAN
SERIES®

COURSE
TECHNOLOGY

COURSE TECHNOLOGY
ONE MAIN STREET
CAMBRIDGE MA 02142

an International Thomson Publishing company I(T)P®

CAMBRIDGE   ALBANY   BONN   CINCINNATI   LONDON   MADRID   MELBOURNE

MEXICO CITY   NEW YORK   PARIS   SAN FRANCISCO   TOKYO   TORONTO   WASHINGTON

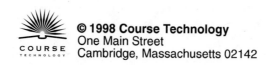

© 1998 Course Technology
One Main Street
Cambridge, Massachusetts 02142

International Thomson Publishing
The ITP logo is a registered trademark
of International Thomson Publishing.

Printed in the United States of America

For more information, contact Course Technology:

Course Technology
One Main Street
Cambridge, Massachusetts 02142, USA

International Thomson Publishing Europe
Berkshire House
168-173 High Holborn
London, WC1V 7AA, United Kingdom

Thomas Nelson Australia
102 Dodds Street
South Melbourne
Victoria 3205 Australia

Nelson Canada
1120 Birchmont Road
Scarborough, Ontario
Canada M1K 5G4

International Thomson Editores
Campos Eliseos 385, Piso 7
Colonia Polanco
11560 Mexico D.F. Mexico

International Thomson Publishing GmbH
Konigswinterer Strasse 418
53227 Bonn, Germany

International Thomson Publishing Asia
Block 211, Henderson Road #08-03
Henderson Industrial Park
Singapore 0315

International Thomson Publishing Japan
Hirakawa-cho Kyowa Building, 3F
2-2-1 Hirakawa-cho, Chiyoda-ku
Tokyo 102, Japan

ISBN 0-7895-1277-7

PHOTO CREDITS: *Project 1, pages NC 1.4-5*, Serious eye, images © 1997 PhotoDisc, Inc.; *Project 2, pages NC 2.2-3*, Tim Berners-Lee,
Courtesy of Tim Berners-Lee/MIT; globe, Courtesy of Corel Professional Photos CD-ROM Image usage; *Project 3, pages NC 3.2-3*,
Smetana, provided by Tony Stone Images/Hulton-Getty; violin, Courtesy of Corel Professional Photos CD-ROM Image usage.

2 3 4 5 6 7 8 9 10   BC   2 1 0 9 8

NETSCAPE *Composer*

CREATING WEB PAGES

C O N T E N T S

Preface

The Shelly Cashman Series® Web-browser books reinforce the fact that you made the right choice when you use a Shelly Cashman Sereies book. Earlier Shelly Cashman Series Web-browser books were used by more schools and more students than any other series in text-book publishing. Yet the Shelly Cashman Series team wanted to produce an even better book for Netscape Composer, so the step-by-step pedagogy was refined to present material in an even easier to understand format and with more project-ending activities. Features such as Other Ways and More About were added and enhanced to give students in-depth knowledge. The opening of each project provides a fascinating perspective of the subject covered in the project. Completely redesigned student assignments include the unique Cases and Places. This book provides the finest educational experience for a student learning how to access information and do research using the World Wide Web.

The World Wide Web

In just eight years since its birth, the World Wide Web, or Web for short, has grown beyond all expectations. During this short period of time, the Web has increased from a limited number of networked computers to more than twenty million computers offering hundreds of millions of Web pages on any topic you can imagine. Schools, businesses, and the computing industry all are taking advantage of the Internet to provide products, services, and education electronically.

Web pages do not just happen. Someone must create them using HTML (Hypertext Markup Language). You have the option of creating a Web page by coding directly in HTML or by using a higher-level tool, such as Netscape Composer.

Educational and charitable nonprofit institutions can obtain Netscape Composer for classroom use without cost by downloading Netscape Communicator from the Netscape site at www.netscape.com. For more information, call 1-415-528-2555.

Objectives of This Textbook

Netscape Composer: Creating Web Pages is intended for use in combination with other books in an introductory computer concepts or applications course. This book also is suitable for use in a one-credit hour course or a continuing education course. Specific objectives of this book are as follows:

▶ To expose students to creating Web pages

▶ To teach students how to use Netscape Composer

▶ To encourage curiosity and independent exploration of World Wide Web resources

▶ To develop an exercise-oriented approach that allows students to learn by example

▶ To encourage independent study and help those who are learning about the Internet on their own in a distance education environment

Organization of This Textbook

Netscape Composer: Creating Web Pages consists of three projects that introduce students to creating Web pages. Neither World Wide Web nor Internet experience is necessary. Each project begins with a statement of objectives. The topics in the project are presented in a step-by-step, screen-by-screen manner.

Each project ends with a Project Summary and a section titled What You Should Know. Questions and exercises are presented at the end of each project. Exercises include Test Your Knowledge, Use Help, Apply Your Knowledge, In the Lab, and Cases and Places. The projects are organized as follows:

Project 1 – Creating Web Pages with HTML and the Netscape Page Wizard In Project 1, students are introduced to HTML and the Netscape Page Wizard. After learning the basics of HTML, students create a Web page by writing HTML code with a text editor. The HTML file is saved locally and viewed with Netscape. Students then create a Web page with similar content using the Netscape Page Wizard. Page Wizard is used to enhance the appearance of the second page. The page is saved locally and viewed with Netscape.

Project 2 – Creating Web Pages from Templates and Remote Documents In Project 2, students are introduced to issues of copyright and learn the basic features of Netscape Composer. Students set Composer preferences. After opening a remote template document and saving it locally, it is edited. Students add, delete, search and replace, and cut, copy, and paste text in a document. Students apply character and paragraph formatting features. Linked targets are added to the page. After editing the template, it is saved and tested.

Project 3 – Creating and Publishing Custom Web Pages In Project 3, students are introduced to Web page design. The project covers more sophisticated Composer features such as creating a page texture, using tables, inserting and editing images, and creating hyperlinks from text and images. Students learn more ways to interact with Composer through its various property dialog boxes. Students learn how to use the drag and drop capability of Composer. JavaScript is introduced. A Web page is created from a blank document, saved, tested, and published on the World Wide Web.

End-of-Project Student Activities

A notable strength of the Shelly Cashman Series Web-browser books is the extensive student activities at the end of each project. Well-structured student activities can make the difference between students merely participating in a class and students retaining the information they learn. The following activities are included in this book.

▶ **What You Should Know** A listing of the tasks completed within a project together with the pages where the step-by-step, screen-by-screen explanations appear. This section provides a perfect study review for students.

▶ **Test Your Knowledge** Four pencil-and-paper activities designed to determine the students' understanding of the material in the project. Included are true/false questions, multiple-choice questions, and two short-answer activities.

▶ **Use Help** Any user of Netscape Composer must know how to use Help. Therefore, this book contains two Use Help exercises per project.

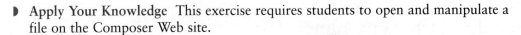

▶ **Apply Your Knowledge** This exercise requires students to open and manipulate a file on the Composer Web site.

▶ **In the Lab** Several in-depth assignments per project require students to apply the knowledge gained in the project to solve problems on a computer.

▶ **Cases and Places** Seven unique case studies require students to apply their knowledge to real-world situations.

Instructor's Resource Kit

A comprehensive Instructor's Resource Kit (IRK) accompanies this textbook in the form of a CD-ROM. The CD-ROM includes an electronic Instructor's Manual (called ElecMan) and teaching and testing aids. The CD-ROM (ISBN 0-7895-1278-5) is available through your Course Technology representative or by calling one of the following telephone numbers: Colleges and Universities, 1-800-648-7450; High Schools, 1-800-824-5179; and Career Colleges, 1-800-477-3692. The contents of the CD-ROM are listed below.

▶ **ElecMan** (*Electronic Instructor's Manual*) ElecMan is made up of Microsoft Word files. The files include lecture notes, solutions to laboratory assignments, and a large test bank. The files allow you to modify the lecture notes or generate quizzes and exams from the test bank using your own word processor. Where appropriate, solutions to laboratory assignments are embedded as icons in the files. When an icon appears, double-click it and the application will start and the solution will display on the screen. ElecMan includes the following for each project: project objectives; project overview; detailed lesson plans with page number references; teacher notes and activities; answers to the end-of-project exercises; test bank of 110 questions for every project (50 true/false, 25 multiple choice, and 35 fill-in-the-blank) with page number references; and transparency references. The transparencies are available through the Figures on CD-ROM described below.

▶ **Figures on CD-ROM** Illustrations for every screen in the textbook are available. Use this ancillary to create a slide show from the illustrations for lecture or to print transparencies for use in lecture with an overhead projector.

▶ **Course Test Manager** Course Test Manager is a powerful testing and assessment package that enables instructors to create and print tests from test banks designed specifically for Course Technology titles. In addition, instructors with access to a networked computer lab (LAN) can administer, grade, and track tests online. Students also can take online practice tests, which generate customized study guides that indicate where in the text students can find more information on each question.

▶ **Lecture Success System** Lecture Success System files are for use with the application software, a personal computer, and projection device to explain and illustrate the step-by-step, screen-by-screen development of a project in the textbook without entering large amounts of data.

▶ **Interactive Labs** Eighteen hands-on interactive labs that take students from ten to fifteen minutes each to step through help solidify and reinforce mouse and keyboard usage and computer concepts.

Shelly Cashman Online

Shelly Cashman Online is a World Wide Web service available to instructors and students of computer education. Visit Shelly Cashman Online at www.scseries.com.

▶ **Series Information** Information on the Shelly Cashman Series products.

▶ **The Community** Opportunities to discuss your course and your ideas with instructors in your field and with the Shelly Cashman Series team.

▶ **Teaching Resources** Designed for instructors teaching from and using Shelly Cashman Series textbooks and software. This area includes password-protected instructor materials that can be downloaded, course outlines, teaching tips, and much more.

▶ **Student Center** Dedicated to students learning about computers with Shelly Cashman Series textbooks and software. This area includes cool links, data from Data Disks that can be downloaded, and much more.

In addition, the Web site www.scsite.com/nc contains URLs for more in-depth study of many of the topics referenced in the More About features as well as page templates and clip art images used in the projects and end-of-project exercises.

Acknowledgments

The Shelly Cashman Series would not be the leading computer education series without the contributions of outstanding publishing professionals. First, and foremost, among them is Becky Herrington, director of production and designer. She is the heart and soul of the Shelly Cashman Series, and it is only through her leadership, dedication, and tireless efforts that superior products are made possible. Becky created and produced the award-winning Windows 95 series of books.

Under Becky's direction, the following individuals made significant contributions to these books: Peter Schiller, production manager; Ginny Harvey, series specialist and developmental editor; Ken Russo, Mike Bodnar, Stephanie Nance, Greg Herrington, and Dave Bonnewitz, graphic artists; Jeanne Black, Quark expert; Patti Koosed, editorial assistant; Nancy Lamm, Marilyn Martin, Lyn Markowicz, Cherilyn King, and Steve Marconi, proofreaders; Cristina Haley, indexer; Sarah Evertson of Image Quest, photo researcher; and Peggy Wyman and Jerry Orton, Susan Sebok, and Nancy Lamm, contributing writers.

Special thanks go to Jim Quasney, our dedicated series editor; Lisa Strite, senior product manager; Lora Wade, associate product manager; Scott MacDonald and Tonia Grafakos, editorial assistants; and Sarah McLean, product marketing manager.
Special mention must go to Suzanne Biron, Becky Herrington, and Michael Gregson for the outstanding book design; Becky Herrington for the cover design; and Ken Russo for the cover illustrations.

Gary B. Shelly
Thomas J. Cashman
John F. Repede

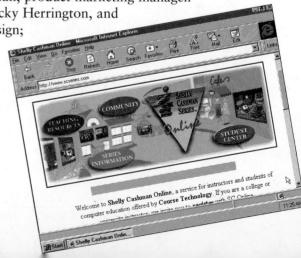

Netscape Composer

Netscape Composer

Creating Web Pages with HTML and the Netscape Page Wizard

Objectives:

You will have mastered the material in this project when you can:

▶ Identify common Web page elements
▶ View a document's source
▶ Describe HTML
▶ Explain the use of basic HTML tags
▶ Create a Web page with a text editor
▶ Explain the purpose of HTML editors
▶ Create a Web page with the Netscape Page Wizard
▶ Save a Web page locally
▶ Print a Web page from Composer

THE COMPLETE *AUTHORING TOOL* FOR WEB PAGES

At first glance, the best-selling authors Alan Ginsberg, Ernest Hemingway, and Alex Haley appear to have little in common. Each wrote unique works for distinct audiences at certain historical moments. Yet, despite the apparent differences, these authors have at least one common trait: editors had the final say in the design of their books.

Would-be authors of World Wide Web pages have the best of both worlds: they are writers *and* editors of their own work.

In traditional publishing, an author writes a manuscript and an editor *marks up* the pages with instructions for layout. The designer, in conjunction with the markups, lays out the pages accordingly. Adjustments are made by the editor and author, and the designer revises the layout until it is complete.

In Web publishing, the author writes a text file and marks up the words with special HTML (hyper-text markup language) character sequences, called tags, to indicate the various formatting features. HTML tags begin and end with brackets (< and >) and usually come in pairs to indicate the beginning and ending of a formatting feature such as headings, bulleted lists, placement of inline images, links to other pages, and more.

HTML is not a programming language; it is a coding scheme that can be interpreted by a Web browser, such as Netscape Navigator. As an HTML document stored on an Internet server, a Web page can be retrieved and displayed on a computer with a Web browser. The HTML tags specify how the Web page displays and indicates links to other documents. These links to other documents are called hyperlinks. Hyperlinks can be text, graphics, sound, or other media. Text links, which are most common, are known as hypertext.

Creating Web pages by writing HTML can be tedious and confusing, but a basic understanding of the process is valuable. HTML editors, also called Web page editors, or Web authoring tools, are applications that allow you to create Web pages in an environment similar to word processing. You create the page in an edit window where formatting features look very close to the way they appear in your browser.

The document creation capabilities of Composer are designed to provide both experienced and beginning content creators with a simple yet powerful solution for editing and publishing online documents.

This project illustrates using the Page Wizard to produce a Web page. Page Wizard is an easy-to-use online HTML editor that eliminates the need to write the HTML tags. The Page Wizard is a special page on the Netscape home site that walks you through the steps for creating a Web page. When you have completed the steps, you will have a page that you can open in Composer and continue building on as your skills improve.

While your work may not win a Pulitzer Prize, as an aspiring Web page author, you have a distinct advantage over the literary authors: playing every cast of characters, from author to editor to designer.

Project

Netscape Composer

Creating Web Pages with HTML and the Netscape Page Wizard

Case Perspective

John Robbins is a friend of yours from school. John recently has obtained an account on the school's Web server and he would like to have his own Web page. John is familiar with the World Wide Web and Netscape Navigator, but when it comes to creating Web pages, he is clueless. John has come to you for help.

In his travels through the Web, John has seen pages that use elements such as color, animated graphics, tables, frames, and sound in very effective and engaging ways. He also has seen these same elements overused and misused, resulting in pages that are ineffective and distracting. Because of this, his expectations for his first Web page are modest.

John would like his first Web page to contain some information about himself, links to some of his favorite sites on the Web, and a way for people to send him email.

Introduction

When you type a URL, click a bookmark, or click a link, you are instructing Netscape Navigator to request a file from a Web server. Although Web browsers such as Netscape Navigator are capable of displaying some very dramatic looking Web pages, the page exists on the Web server and is received by the browser as nothing more than a text file.

What Is HTML?

Although a Web page exists as a text file, the text file must contain formatting instructions for the browser to use when it displays the page. The standard language used to write these formatting instructions for Web pages is the **HyperText Markup Language (HTML)**.

In this project, you will learn the basics of HTML, and you will learn how to view any Web page's HTML file. You will create a Web page by writing the content and HTML instructions using a simple text editor application.

What Is Netscape Composer?

Creating Web pages by writing HTML can be tedious and confusing. Fortunately, editor programs are available that write the HTML instructions for you. Netscape Communications Corporation's Navigator is the world's most popular Web browser. In addition to the features of Navigator, Netscape Communicator includes a Web page editor called Composer. Composer provides an environment similar to a word processor through which Web pages can be created quickly and easily.

In this project, you will learn about Web page editors and the Netscape Page Wizard. You will use the **Page Wizard** to create a Web page (Figure 1-1) whose appearance is very similar to the one you will have created using the text editor. You will learn some of the advantages and limitations of Web page editors.

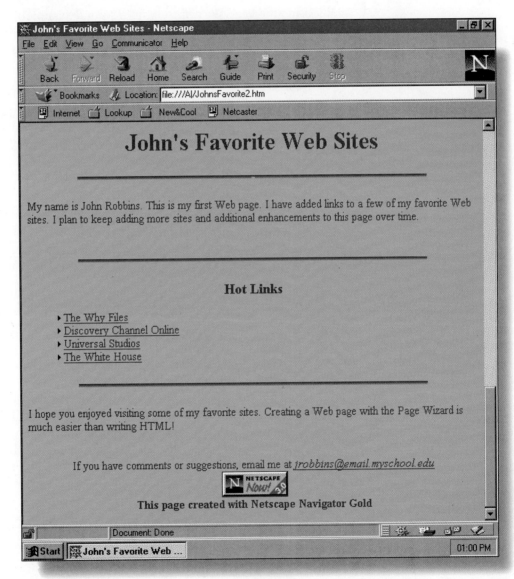

FIGURE 1-1

Project One — John's Favorite Web Sites

After talking with John, you have a good idea of the desired content and appearance of John's first Web page. Prior to creating the Web page, John's Favorite Web Sites, you must sketch it (see Figure 1-11 on page NC 1.16). Before you produce this page for him using the Microsoft Notepad text editor, however, you will have to learn the basics of HTML.

Mary Cunningham, another friend from school, has mentioned how easy it is to create Web pages with the Netscape Page Wizard. You will test Mary's claim by using the Page Wizard to build a second version of John's Favorite Web Sites. You then can determine for yourself the advantages and limitations of the Page Wizard.

Project Steps

The following tasks will be completed in this project.

1. View a document's source.
2. Start Notepad.
3. Create a Web page with a text editor (Notepad).
4. Save the Web page source file.
5. View and test the file.
6. Start Page Wizard.
7. Add content to a page with the Page Wizard.
8. Adjust the page's appearance with Page Wizard.
9. Build and save the file.
10. View and test the Web page.

Understanding HTML

A **markup language** uses special sequences of characters within a document to control what the document looks like when it is displayed on a screen or printed. One example of a markup language is Microsoft's RTF (rich text format), which is used by word processing applications to control formatting features such as a bulleted list of objectives. Because Web pages exist only as text files, a markup language must be used to instruct Web browsers how to format and display the page. The **HyperText Markup Language (HTML)** is the standard markup language used in creating Web pages. HTML itself continues to evolve, incorporating more and more sophisticated formatting features. Standards for HTML are set by an organization called the **World Wide Web Consortium.**

Web Page Elements

Although Web pages can be as distinctive and different as the individuals who create them, a relatively small set of basic features, or elements, are common to most Web pages. As you begin to look at Web pages through the eyes of a Web page creator, you will notice that most pages are variations on the use of the elements identified in Figure 1-2 on page NC 1.9 and Figure 1-3 on page NC 1.10.

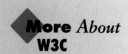

More About
W3C

The World Wide Web Consortium (W3C) is an international industry consortium founded in 1994 to develop common protocols for the evolution of the World Wide Web. For more information on the World Wide Web Consortium (W3C), visit the Composer Web site (www.scsite.com/nc/pr1.htm) and click the link to W3C.

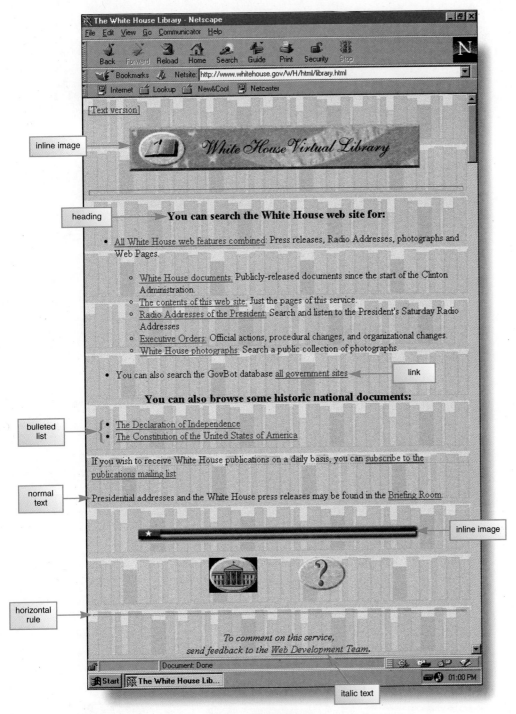

FIGURE 1-2

The **title** of a Web page is the text that appears on the title bar of the Netscape window when the page is being displayed. The **background** of a Web page is similar to the wallpaper in Windows. It provides a backdrop against which the other elements are shown. The background can be either a solid color or a small graphic image that is **tiled**, or repeated, across the entire page. **Normal text** is the text that makes up the main information content of a Web page. Normal text also can be formatted to bold, italic, underlined, or different colors. **Headings** are used to set off different paragraphs of text or different sections of a page. Headings are a larger font size than normal text and usually are bold.

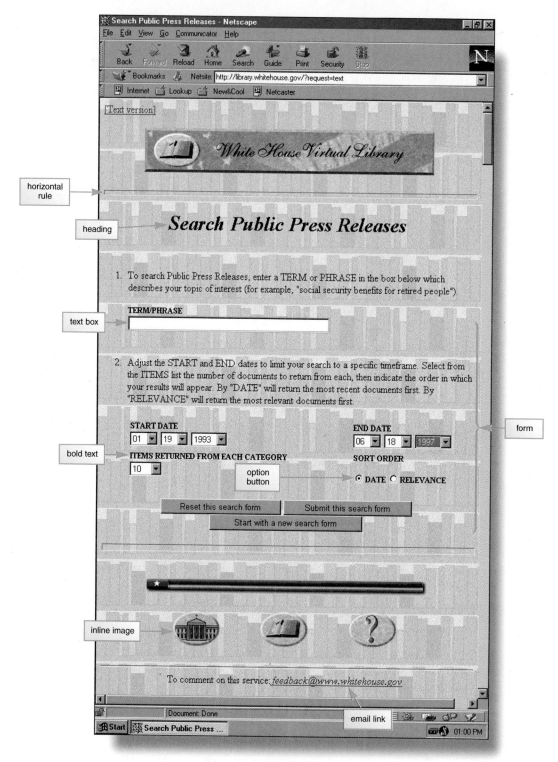

FIGURE 1-3

Inline images are graphics and pictures that are contained within the page as it is displayed. Inline images are not part of the page's HTML file itself, but are contained in separate files. The HTML file contains **tags**, which are special characters that tell the browser which graphic file to request from the server, where to locate it on the page, and how to display it. Some inline images are **animated**, changing their appearance over time. An **image map** is a special type of inline image, where clicking different areas of the graphic instructs the browser to display a different area of the current page or a different page altogether.

Links are areas of the page that when clicked cause the browser to request another file from a server. Links to other files are not limited to Web page files and commonly include external graphics, sound, multimedia, and program files. Text, inline images, and image maps are commonly used for links. When text is used as a link, it is given a color different from the normal text. **Horizontal rules** are lines that appear across the page to separate different sections of the page. Although the appearance of horizontal rules vary, it is common for a horizontal bar on a Web page actually to be an inline image.

Many Web pages present a series of text items as a **list**. Lists can be **numbered**, or can have **bullets** (small images) preceding each item. Different shapes of bullets are available, but just as with the horizontal rules, many Web pages actually use inline images for the bullets. **Forms** are areas of a Web page where the person visiting the page can enter information to be sent back to the server. The information is supplied using input elements within the form such as option buttons and text boxes. **Tables** are used to present text in rows and columns. The intersection of a row and column is called a **cell**. The text in a cell often is used as a link. The borderwidth of a table determines the width of the grid lines surrounding the cells. When the borderwidth is set to zero, grid lines do not display.

HTML Basics

HTML uses special character sequences, called **tags**, to indicate the various formatting features. Tags begin with the less than sign, <, and end with the greater than sign >. Tags usually come in pairs to indicate the beginning and end of a formatting feature. The end tag contains a slash /. For example, <H1> indicates the beginning of a size 1 (largest) heading , and </H1> indicates the end of that format. These tags would be used to display the text, John's Favorite Web Sites, as a size 1 heading as follows:

<H1>John's Favorite Web Sites</H1>

Tags can be used in combination to apply multiple formatting features at the same time. For example,

<CENTER><H1>John's Favorite Web Sites</H1></CENTER>

would center the size 1 heading on the page. In the example above, you can see that when tags are used in combination, the closing tags are in the opposite order as the beginning tags.

Many HTML tags also can contain **keywords** that further define the appearance of the element created by the tag. Keywords take the form keyword=value. For example, ALIGN=CENTER tells the browser to center text on the page and can be used within the <H1> tag as follows:

<H1 ALIGN=CENTER>John's Favorite Web Sites</H1>

Every element of every Web page you have ever viewed has corresponding tags. Some of the more commonly used tags are described in Table 1-1 on the next page.

More *About* **HTML**

HTML has been in use by the World Wide Web (WWW) global information initiative since 1990 and undergoes review and revision constantly. For more information on the most recent specification of HTML, visit the Composer Web site (www.scsite.com/nc/pr1.htm) and click the link to HTML.

Two of the more frequently used tags are those for creating a link and inserting an inline image. Links are added with the <A> </A> tag. The HREF (hypertext reference) keyword and the URL (in quotation marks) of the file that is being linked to are included within the tag. The text in between the beginning link tag and the ending link tag becomes the underlined text on the Web page that is clicked to initiate the link, called hypertext. For example, to create a link to Netscape's Amazing Fishcam page with the hypertext Amazing Fishcam, you would type <A HREF="http://www2.netscape.com/fishcam/fishcam.html"> Amazing Fishcam</A>.

An inline image is inserted in a Web page with the <IMG> tag. The **SRC** keyword and the URL (in quotation marks) of the graphic file being inserted are included within the tag. For example, <IMG SRC="mypicture.gif"> would insert a graphic with the file name mypicture.gif.

If only the name of the file is supplied after the HREF or SRC keywords, as in the preceding example, the browser will look for that file on the Web server and in the directory where the current Web page is located. If both a path and file name are specified (for example, <IMG SRC="/images/mypicture.gif">), then the browser will look in the specified path on the Web server where the current page is located. Additionally, a file on another Web server can be specified by including a complete URL, such as <IMG SRC="http://www.myschool.edu/images/mypicture.gif">

Viewing a Document's Source

A Web page commonly is referred to as a **document**, to distinguish it from other types of files such as sound files or graphic files. The text file containing the content and HTML tags for a particular Web page is referred to as the page's **HTML file, source file,** or **document source.** Netscape Navigator allows you to display the document source for any Web page in a separate window. This is especially useful when you see something interesting on a Web page and want to know the HTML code behind it. Complete the following steps to start Netscape Navigator and see the HTML code that creates the White House home page.

Table 1-1	
HTML TAG	*FUNCTION*
<HTML> </HTML>	Indicates the beginning and end of an HTML document
<HEAD> </HEAD>	Indicates the beginning and end of a section of the document used for the title and other document header information
<TITLE> </TITLE>	Indicates the beginning and end of the title: the title does not display on the Web page, but appears in the title bar of the browser
<BODY> </BODY>	Indicates the beginning and end of the main section of the Web page (as opposed to the head)
<H1> </H1>	Indicates the beginning and end of a section of text called a heading; font size is larger than normal text; sizes for headings are integers from 1 to 6 (1 is largest; 6 is smallest)
<P>	Indicates the beginning of a new paragraph; inserts a blank line above the new paragraph
<B> </B>	Indicates the beginning and end of a section of bold text
<I> </I>	Indicates the beginning and end of a section of italic text
<BLINK> </BLINK>	Indicates the beginning and end of a section of blinking text
<CENTER> </CENTER>	Causes the text or graphic specified between these tags to be centered on the page
<HR>	Inserts a horizontal rule
<UL> </UL>	Indicates the beginning and end of an unordered (bulleted) list of items
<LI>	Indicates the item that follows the tag is an item within a list
<A> </A>	Indicates the beginning and end of a link
<IMG>	Inserts an inline image into the page

Steps **To View a Document's Source**

1 **Point to the Netscape Communicator shortcut icon on the desktop (Figure 1-4).**

Your desktop may have a different arrangement of shortcut icons.

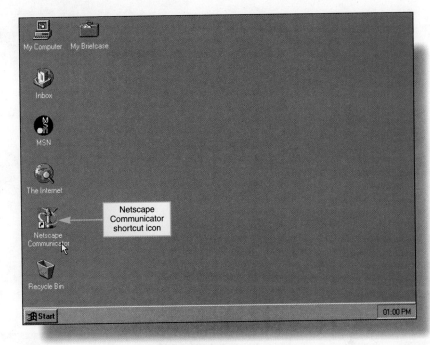

FIGURE 1-4

2 **Double-click the Netscape Communicator shortcut icon.**

Netscape Navigator opens on the desktop (Figure 1-5). Your system may be configured to display a different startup page.

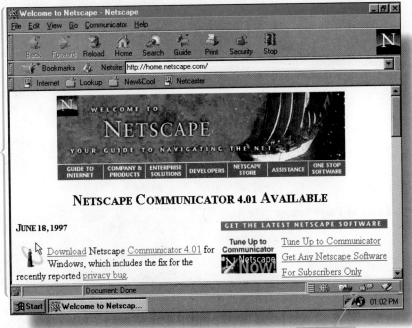

FIGURE 1-5

3 **In the Location text box, type www.whitehouse.gov and then press the ENTER key.**

The White House home page displays (Figure 1-6).

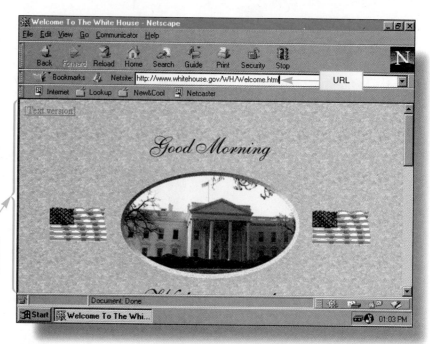

Web page displays in browser

URL

FIGURE 1-6

4 **Click View on the menu bar.**

The View menu displays (Figure 1-7).

View menu

FIGURE 1-7

5 **Point to Page Source (Figure 1-8)**

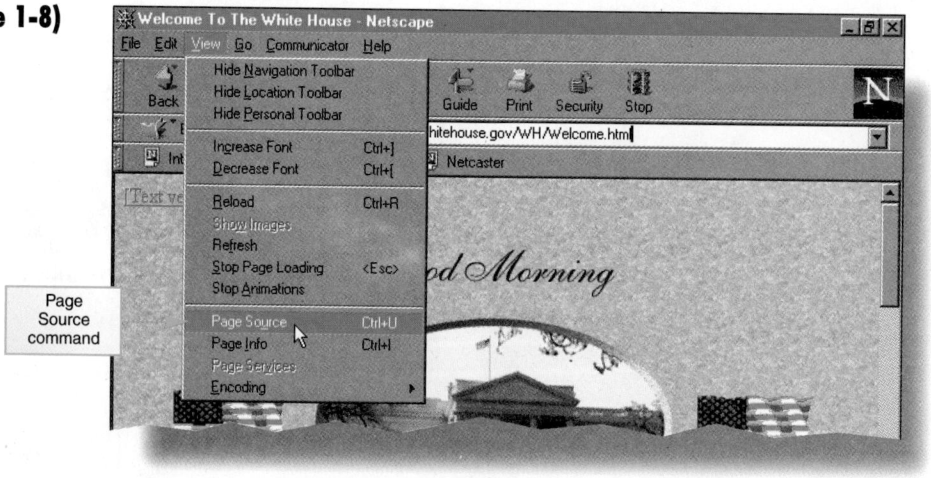

Page Source command

FIGURE 1-8

6 **Click Page Source.**

The HTML (source) file displays in the Netscape document source window (Figure 1-9).

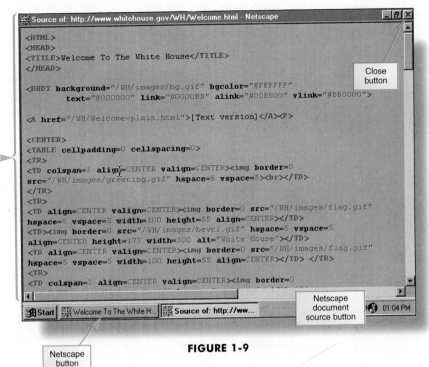

FIGURE 1-9

7 **Try to identify some of the tags in the Netscape document source window. Click the Netscape document source window's Close button.**

The Netscape document source window closes (Figure 1-10).

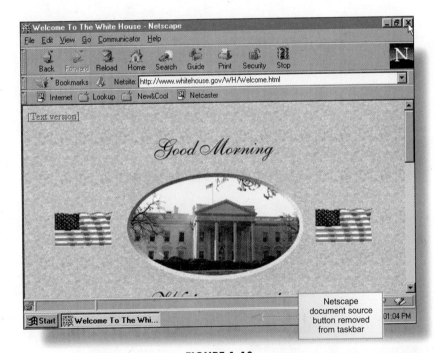

FIGURE 1-10

In the preceding steps, you clicked Page Source on the View menu to open the document source window. In addition to viewing the HTML code, you can copy a section of the code to the Clipboard by dragging through the section to be copied and then pressing the CTRL+C keys. The code then is available on the Windows Clipboard and can be pasted into your own HTML file.

Other Ways

1. Right-click anywhere on Web page, click View Source on pop-up menu

Creating a Web Page with a Text Editor

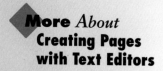
Web page files contain the page's content and the HTML formatting instructions as plain text. For this reason, any text editor can be used to create a Web page. In the following steps, you will use the Microsoft Windows Notepad application.

HTML is not case-sensitive; therefore, tags and keywords can be either uppercase or lowercase. You must be careful with file names contained in links, however, because file names are case-sensitive on some Web servers. In the steps that follow, you will use all uppercase. Web browsers ignore any formatting of the HTML file itself, such as indents, blank lines, and line breaks. To the browser, the file is just one long, continuous string of characters. For example, an HTML file that begins

```
<HTML>
<HEAD>
<TITLE>John's Favorite Web Sites</TITLE>
</HEAD>
```

will be treated by the browser exactly the same as a file that begins

```
<HTML><HEAD><TITLE>John's Favorite Web Sites</TITLE></HEAD>
```

It does, however, make it easier for you to write and read the HTML file if you include line breaks and indents. In the following steps, you will write the content and HTML tags for John's Favorite Web Sites page using the sketch in Figure 1-11. The steps are grouped by sections of John's page as shown in the sketch.

Opening a New HTML File

Similar to many word processors, Notepad opens a new file for you to edit each time you start Notepad. To start Notepad, Windows 95 must be running. Perform the following steps to start Notepad and open a new HTML file for editing.

centered
heading (large)
and horizontal rule →

John's Favorite Web Sites

normal text,
horizontal rule, and
centered heading
(medium) →

My name is John Robbins...
(some other text here)

HOT LINKS

bulleted list
of links →

☆ *The WHY Files*
☆ *Discovery Channel Online*
☆ *Universal Studios*
☆ *The White House*

} *hyper links
to these pages*

horizontal rule,
normal text,
and link →

(some closing text here ...)

You can email me at John Robbins

↑
(email link)

FIGURE 1-11

TO ADD NORMAL TEXT AND CENTER A HEADING WITH THE ALIGN KEYWORD

1 Type <P>My name is John Robbins. This is my first Web page. I have added links and then press the ENTER key.

2 Type to a few of my favorite Web sites. I plan to keep adding more sites and and then press the ENTER key.

3 Type additional enhancements to this page over time. and then press the ENTER key.

4 Type <P><HR> and then press the ENTER key.

5 Type <H3 ALIGN=CENTER>Hot Links</H3> and then press the ENTER key.

Your HTML document should display as shown in Figure 1-15.

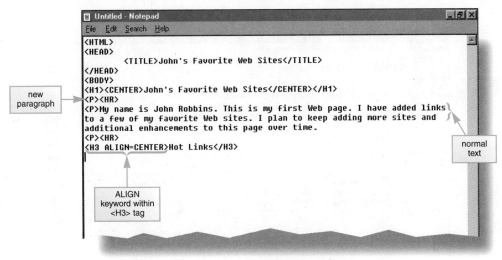

FIGURE 1-15

The line breaks you added by pressing the ENTER key in Step 1 through Step 3 will have no effect on the Web page's appearance. The text you typed will be treated by Netscape the same as if you had typed it all on one line. The width of the browser's window determines where the text will break when it is displayed by the browser. You added the line breaks where you did only so that you could view all of the text without having to scroll the Notepad window.

Adding a Bulleted List and Links to Other Pages with HTML

A list of items on a page where each item is preceded by a **bullet** (small disc, circle, or square) is called an **unordered list**. An unordered list begins and ends with the <UL> and </UL> tags. The bullet can be changed by using the TYPE keyword within the <UL> tag. When no TYPE is specified, the bullet is a solid circle. Each item in the list must be preceded by <LI>, the **list item** tag.

John's page will use an unordered list for the links to John's favorite sites. You should recall from the section on HTML basics that the <A> tag is used to create hyperlinks to other files that are available on the World Wide Web. The hypertext for each link on John's page will be the name of the page being linked to. Perform the steps on the next page to add a bulleted list of links to other Web pages.

TO ADD A BULLETED LIST AND LINKS TO OTHER PAGES WITH HTML

1 Type <UL> and then press the ENTER key.

2 Type <LI><A HREF="http://whyfiles.news.wisc.edu/">The Why Files</A> and then press the ENTER key.

3 Type <LI><A HREF="http://www.discovery.com">Discovery Channel Online</A> and then press the ENTER key.

4 Type <LI><A HREF="http://www.mca.com">Universal Studios</A> and then press the ENTER key.

5 Type <LI><A HREF="http://www.whitehouse.gov">The White House</A> and then press the ENTER key.

6 Type </UL> and then press the ENTER key.

Your HTML document should display as shown in Figure 1-16.

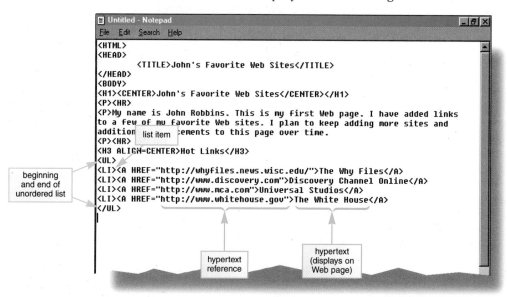

FIGURE 1-16

In the preceding steps, you created an unordered list. An **ordered list** has consecutive numbers in place of the bullets. An ordered list is created in the same way as an unordered list but uses the <OL> and </OL> tags in place of the <UL> and </UL> tags.

Adding Italic Text and an Email Link with HTML

The final section of John's document begins with a horizontal rule to separate it from the list of links. John then wants a concluding paragraph of text and a way for persons viewing the page to email him directly from the page. This type of email link is created in HTML by using the **mailto:** value of the HREF keyword within the <A> link tag. The hypertext for the link will be the email address in italics.

Perform the following steps to conclude the content of John's page by adding italic text and an email link.

TO ADD ITALIC TEXT AND AN EMAIL LINK WITH HTML

1 Type <P><HR> and then press the ENTER key.

2 Type <P>I hope you enjoyed visiting some of my favorite sites. Creating and then press the ENTER key.

③ Type a Web page by writing HTML with a text editor is not rocket science, but and then press the ENTER key.

④ Type there must be easier ways! And then press the ENTER key.

⑤ Type <P><CENTER>If you have comments or suggestions, email me at and then press the ENTER key.

⑥ Type <A HREF="mailto:jrobbins@email.myschool.edu"><I>John Robbins</I></A></CENTER> and then press the ENTER key.

Your HTML document should display as shown in Figure 1-17.

The hypertext for a link can be anything you want it to be. In the preceding steps, the email link hypertext was John's name. On many Web pages, the entire email address is used for the email link hypertext.

Closing and Saving an HTML File

Before you can save the HTML file, you must add the ending tag for the body and the ending tag for the HTML document. You then will save the file on a floppy disk. Perform the following step to close the HTML document and save the file on a floppy disk.

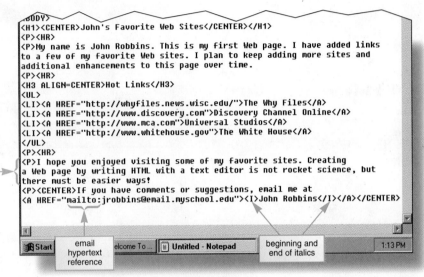

FIGURE 1-17

 Steps **To Close and Save an HTML File**

① **Type** </BODY> **and then press the ENTER key. Type** </HTML> **as the final entry.**

Your HTML document should display as shown in Figure 1-18.

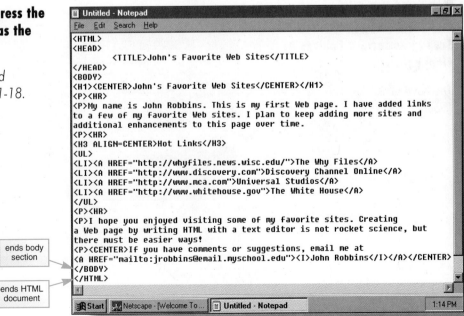

FIGURE 1-18

2 **Click File on Notepad's menu bar. Point to Save As.**

The File menu displays (Figure 1-19).

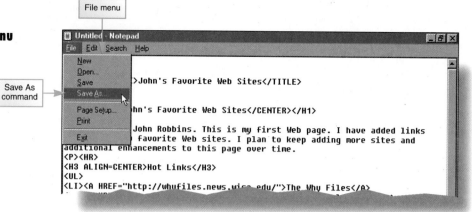

FIGURE 1-19

3 **Click Save As.**

The Save As dialog box opens (Figure 1-20).

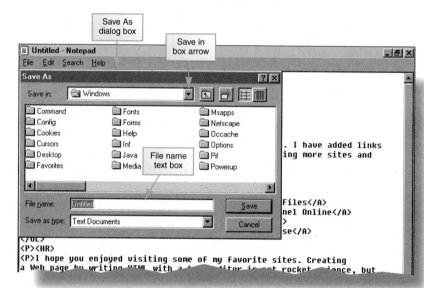

FIGURE 1-20

4 **Type** JohnsFavorite.htm **in the File name text box. Click the Save in box arrow. Point to 3½ Floppy [A:].**

The Save in list box displays (Figure 1-21).

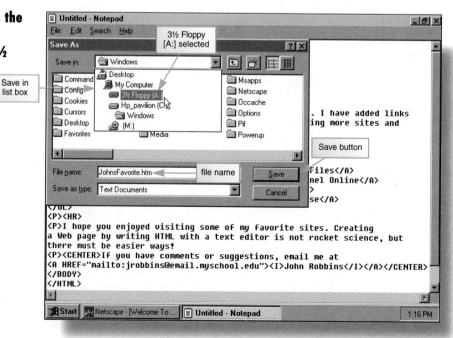

FIGURE 1-21

5 Click 3½ Floppy [A:]. With a formatted floppy disk inserted in drive A, click the Save button.

The file is saved on the floppy disk and the dialog box closes (Figure 1-22).

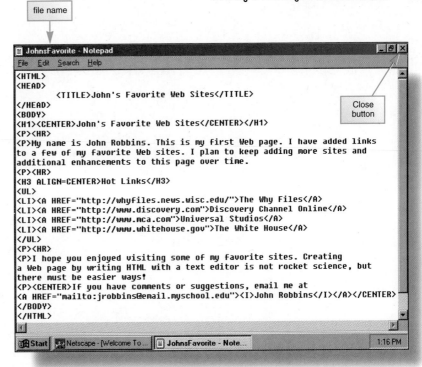

file name

Close button

```
JohnsFavorite - Notepad
File  Edit  Search  Help
<HTML>
<HEAD>
          <TITLE>John's Favorite Web Sites</TITLE>
</HEAD>
<BODY>
<H1><CENTER>John's Favorite Web Sites</CENTER></H1>
<P><HR>
<P>My name is John Robbins. This is my first Web page. I have added links
to a few of my favorite Web sites. I plan to keep adding more sites and
additional enhancements to this page over time.
<P><HR>
<H3 ALIGN=CENTER>Hot Links</H3>
<UL>
<LI><A HREF="http://whyfiles.news.wisc.edu/">The Why Files</A>
<LI><A HREF="http://www.discovery.com">Discovery Channel Online</A>
<LI><A HREF="http://www.mca.com">Universal Studios</A>
<LI><A HREF="http://www.whitehouse.gov">The White House</A>
</UL>
<P><HR>
<P>I hope you enjoyed visiting some of my favorite sites. Creating
a Web page by writing HTML with a text editor is not rocket science, but
there must be easier ways!
<P><CENTER>If you have comments or suggestions, email me at
<A HREF="mailto:jrobbins@email.myschool.edu"><I>John Robbins</I></A></CENTER>
</BODY>
</HTML>
```

Start | Netscape - [Welcome To ... | JohnsFavorite - Note...   1:16 PM

FIGURE 1-22

6 Click the Notepad window's Close button.

The Notepad window closes. Netscape is open on the desktop (Figure 1-23).

Netscape browser window

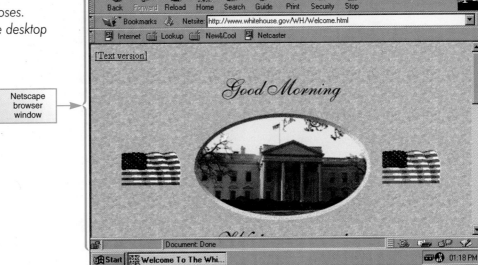

Welcome To The White House - Netscape
File Edit View Go Communicator Help

Back Forward Reload Home Search Guide Print Security Stop

Bookmarks   Netsite: http://www.whitehouse.gov/WH/Welcome.html

Internet   Lookup   New&Cool   Netcaster

[Text version]

Good Morning

Document: Done

Start | Welcome To The Whi...   01:18 PM

FIGURE 1-23

OtherWays

1. Click Notepad Close button, click Yes button, enter appropriate information in Save As dialog box, click Save button in Save As dialog box

In the preceding steps, you completed the HTML file and then saved it **locally**, meaning it was saved on a hard disk or floppy disk that is part of your PC. It also is called a **local document**. If you copied the file to a Web server, the copy would be called a **remote document**.

Viewing and Testing a Local HTML File in Netscape

After you create a page, you should test it before you publish it. It is very easy to make mistakes writing HTML, and you may have to go back and make corrections after viewing the page in the browser. Currently, John's Favorite Web Sites page is available only to you because it is a local file. **Publishing** a page refers to transferring the Web page file (and all associated files such as inline images) to a Web server where the page then is available to the rest of the World Wide Web. Perform the following steps to view and test the JohnsFavorite.htm file within the Netscape browser.

Steps To View and Test a Local HTML File in Netscape

1 **Click File on the menu bar, and then point to Open Page.**

The File menu displays (Figure 1-24).

FIGURE 1-24

2 **Click Open Page.**

The Open Page dialog displays (Figure 1-25).

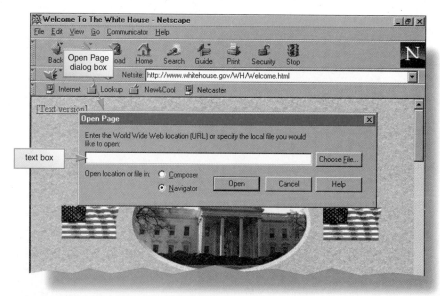

FIGURE 1-25

3 **Type** a:\JohnsFavorite.htm **in the text box and then point to the Open button.**

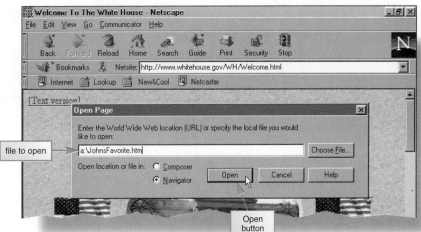

FIGURE 1-26

4 **Click the Open button.**

JohnsFavorite.htm is read by Netscape and displays as shown in Figure 1-27.

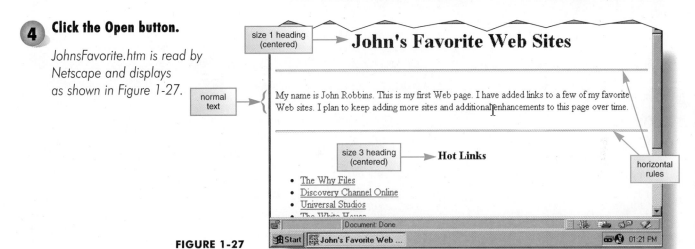

FIGURE 1-27

5 **Scroll down John's page and click Universal Studios.**

The linked page (www.mca.com/) displays in the browser (Figure 1-28)

FIGURE 1-28

6 **Click the Back button on the toolbar. Test the remaining hot links. Click the email link.**

If you have set email preferences, Netscape's Composition window will open (Figure 1-29), otherwise the Netscape dialog box displays.

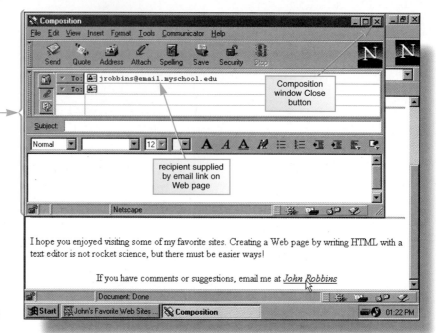

FIGURE 1-29

7 **Click the Close button in the Netscape Composition window or click the OK button in the Netscape dialog box.**

John's page is visible in the browser (Figure 1-30).

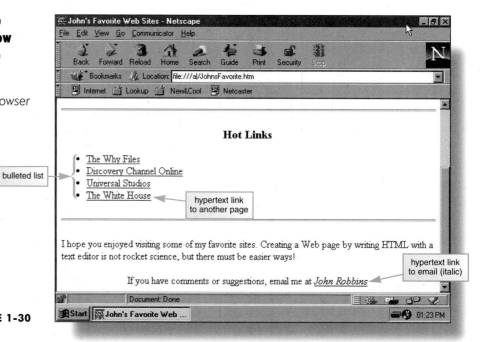

FIGURE 1-30

Other Ways

1. On File menu click Open Page, click Choose File button, enter appropriate information in Open dialog box, click Open button in Open dialog box

Even though JohnsFavorite.htm is a local file, when opened in the browser, it functions the same as if it were on the Web. The next step for John is to **publish** his page (transfer his HTML file to his school's Web server) so it is available to everyone using the Web. The procedures for publishing pages vary greatly because of differences in server hardware, server software, and organizational rules and policies. In many organizations, the person responsible for these is called the **Webmaster.** At this point, John will contact his school's Webmaster for the requirements to publish his page.

What Are HTML Editors and Netscape's Page Wizard?

Writing HTML code for even simple Web pages can be a time-consuming and tedious process. **HTML editors,** also called **Web page editors,** or **Web authoring tools**, are applications that allow you to create Web pages in a word processor-like environment. Pages are created in an editor window where formatting features are displayed in the editor window, similarly to the way they will display in the browser. In the HTML editor, what you see is what you get (WYSIWYG), unlike looking at text and HTML tags in a text editor and trying to visualize in your mind what they will look like in the browser.

Web page editors are not just editors. Their real value is that they are HTML code generators. This means that after you have created the Web page and its elements by pointing and clicking and dragging and dropping, the editor writes the HTML document source automatically. Depending on the complexity of the pages you create and the features of the HTML editor you use, you may never have to write a single HTML tag.

A number of HTML editors are available with varying formatting features and prices. Project 2 and Project 3 of this book discuss and demonstrate Web page creation with Netscape Composer.

The Netscape **Page Wizard** is an easy-to-use, online HTML editor available on the World Wide Web. The tradeoff for this ease of use is that Page Wizard is limited in the Web page layouts and styles that it can create. Nevertheless, the Page Wizard is a valuable tool to begin your understanding of Web page creation with an editor.

> ### More *About* Web Authoring Tools
>
> More than seventy different HTML editors are available for the Windows operating system alone, and an Internet news-group exists devoted just to HTML editors. For more information on HTML editors, visit the Composer Web site (www.scsite.com/nc/pr1.htm) and click the link to HTML Editors.

Creating a Web Page with Netscape's Page Wizard

Now that you have achieved an understanding of HTML by actually writing the HTML code for John's Favorite Web Sites, you will re-create John's Web page using the Page Wizard. You will accomplish this by completing the following tasks.

1. Start Page Wizard.
2. Add a title, heading, and an introduction.
3. Add hot links.
4. Add a conclusion and an email link.
5. Customize the appearance of John's page.
6. Build and save the file.
7. View and test the page.

Starting Page Wizard

To use the Page Wizard, Navigator must be running on the desktop, and you must have an active Internet connection. Perform the steps on the next page to start Page Wizard.

Steps To Start Page Wizard

1 **Click File on the Navigator menu bar, point to New, and point to Page From Wizard.**

The New submenu displays (Figure 1-31).

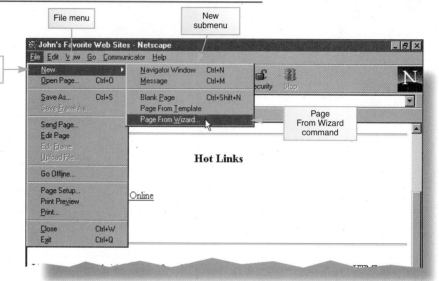

FIGURE 1-31

2 **Click Page From Wizard on the New submenu.**

The Netscape Page Wizard Web page opens. The Page Wizard consists of three frames: the Instructions frame, the Preview frame, and the Choices frame (Figure 1-32).

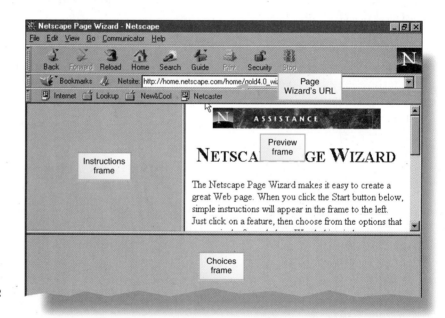

FIGURE 1-32

3 **Scroll to the bottom of the Preview frame and then point to the START button.**

As you build the Web page, Page Wizard will display the page within the Preview frame (Figure 1-33).

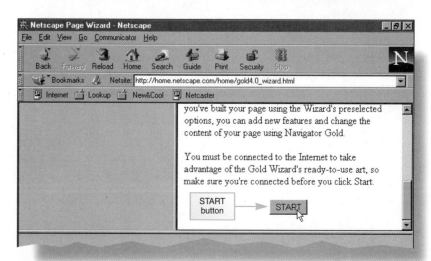

FIGURE 1-33

4 **Click the START button.**

Text displays within the Instructions frame (Figure 1-34).

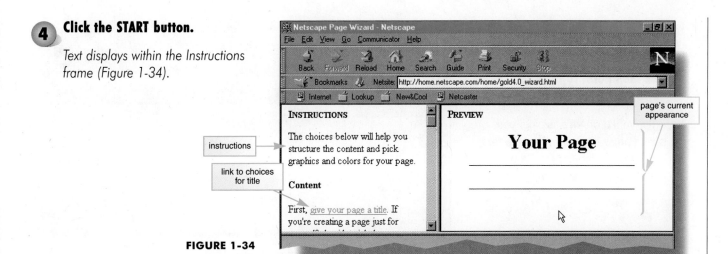

FIGURE 1-34

Other Ways

1. Press ALT+F, press N, press W

The Page Wizard is itself a Web page. You linked to it by clicking Page From Wizard on the New submenu. You also could have opened the Page Wizard page in the browser by typing its URL (home.netscape.com/home/gold3.0_wizard.html) in the Netsite text box and then pressing the ENTER key.

Adding a Title, Heading, and Introduction

In this next set of steps, you will use Page Wizard to add a title, heading, and introduction to the page. When you created this part of John's page with Notepad, you chose to make the heading the same as the title, John's Favorite Web Sites. You could have made them different if you had wanted to. When creating a Web page with the Page Wizard, whatever you choose for the title also will be used for the heading. Perform the following steps to add a title, heading, and introduction to the page.

 Steps **To Add a Title, Heading, and Introduction**

1 **Click give your page a title in the Instructions frame under Content.**

The Title text box displays in the Choices frame (Figure 1-35).

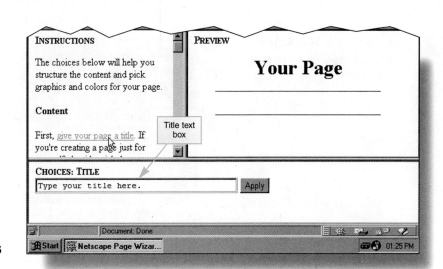

FIGURE 1-35

2 **Drag through the text in the Title text box to highlight it. Type** John's Favorite Web Sites **and then point to the Apply button.**

If you make an error typing, you can change the text in the Title text box by using the BACKSPACE *or* DELETE *key (Figure 1-36).*

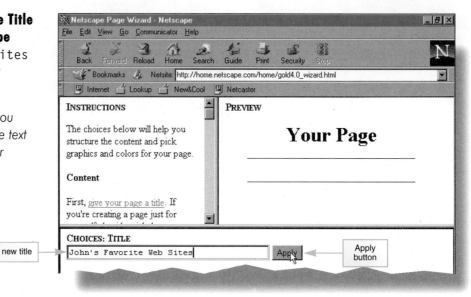

FIGURE 1-36

3 **Click the Apply button.**

The name of the page displays as a size 1 heading on the page in the Preview frame (Figure 1-37).

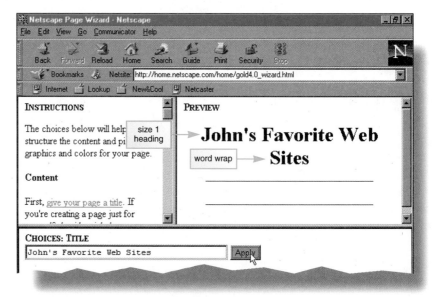

FIGURE 1-37

4 **Scroll down the Instructions frame and then point to type an introduction (Figure 1-38).**

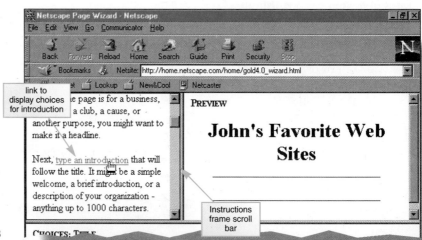

FIGURE 1-38

5 **Click type an introduction.**

The Introduction text box displays in the Choices frame (Figure 1-39).

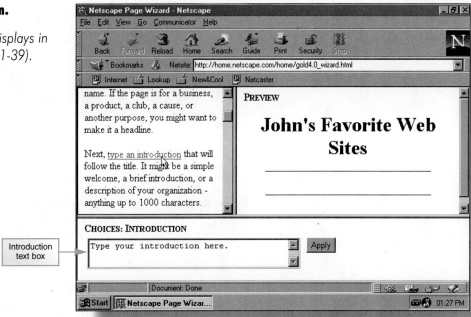

FIGURE 1-39

6 **Drag through the text in the Introduction text box to highlight it. Type (without pressing the ENTER key)** My name is John Robbins. This is my first Web page. I have added links to a few of my favorite Web sites. I plan to keep adding more sites and additional enhancements to this page over time. **Point to the Apply button.**

If you make an error while typing, you can change the text in the Introduction text box. You can scroll the text box to review your introduction text (Figure 1-40).

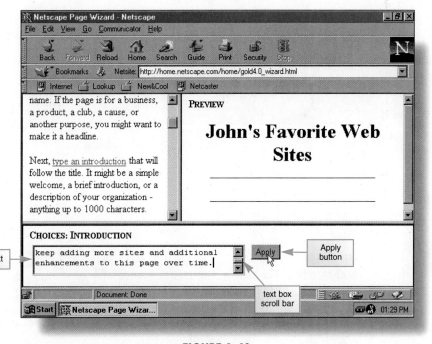

FIGURE 1-40

7 **Click the Apply button and then scroll down the Preview frame to view the introduction.**

The introduction is added to the page and displays in the Preview frame (Figure 1-41).

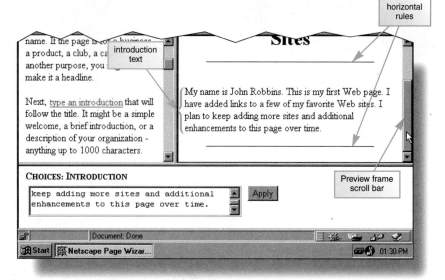

FIGURE 1-41

When you created John's page with Notepad, you added horizontal rules to separate the introduction from the rest of the page. Page Wizard has added those horizontal rules automatically.

Table 1-2	
NAME	URL
The Why Files	http://whyfiles.news.wisc.edu/
Discovery Channel Online	http://www.discovery.com
Universal Studios	http://www.mca.com
The White House	http://www.whitehouse.gov

Adding and Deleting Hot Links

In Notepad, you added links to other pages as list items within an unordered list. Page Wizard automatically displays the links you add as an unordered list. You cannot, however, list the links differently; for example, as an ordered list. Perform the following steps to add the links to the pages listed in Table 1-2.

 To Add Hot Links

1 **Scroll down the Instructions frame. Point to add some hot links to other Web pages (Figure 1-42).**

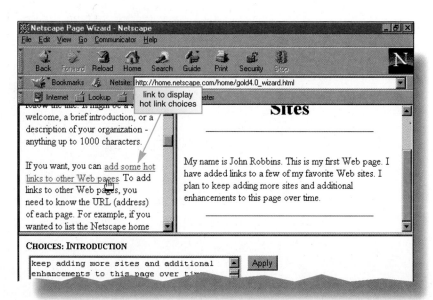

FIGURE 1-42

2 **Click add some hot links to other Web pages.**

The Name and URL text boxes display in the Choices frame (Figure 1-43).

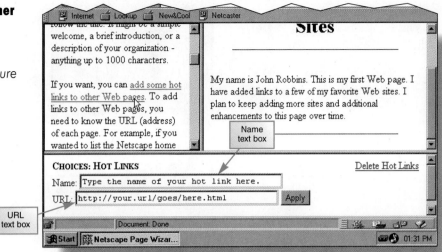

FIGURE 1-43

3 **Drag through the text in the Name text box to highlight it and then type** The Why Files **in the Name text box.**

The name you typed replaces the prompt inside the Name text box (Figure 1-44).

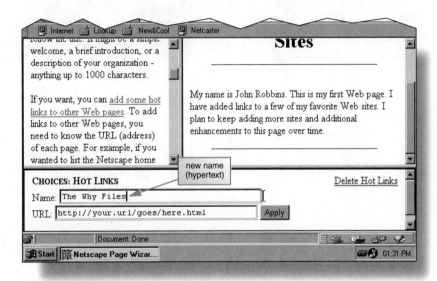

FIGURE 1-44

4 **Drag through the text in the URL text box to highlight it, type** http://whyfiles.news. wisc.edu/ **and point to the Apply button.**

The URL you typed replaces the prompt inside the URL text box (Figure 1-45).

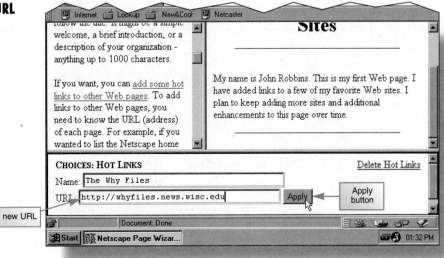

FIGURE 1-45

5 Click the Apply button. Scroll down the Preview frame to view the hyperlink.

The hot link you typed is added to a bulleted list, and a horizontal rule is added below the list (Figure 1-46).

FIGURE 1-46

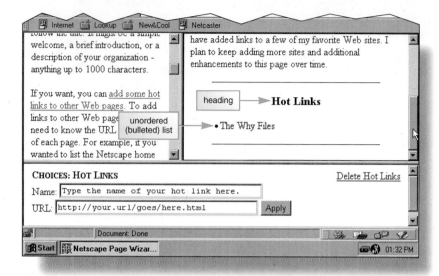

6 Repeat Steps 4 through 6, three times, to add the remaining hot links listed in Table 1-2, on page NC 1.32, and then scroll down to the bottom of the page in the Preview frame.

The bulleted list of links displays in the Preview frame (Figure 1-47).

FIGURE 1-47

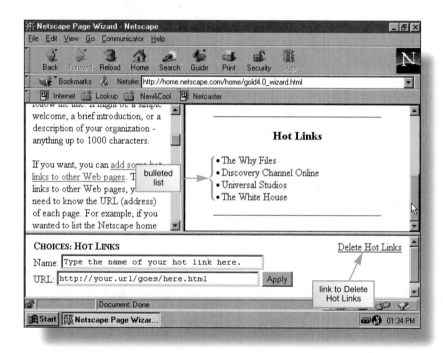

To delete hot links, click Delete Hot Links in the Choices frame. From the list of hot links that displays, uncheck those you wish to delete. They are removed automatically from the page. After deleting links, you can add additional links by clicking Add Hot Links in the Choices frame.

Adding a Conclusion and an Email Link

The last steps in adding the content to John's page consist of a adding a paragraph of concluding text and adding the email link. Although the hypertext for an email link can be anything you want, it is common in Web page development to use the email address as the hypertext. Perform the following steps to add the concluding text and the email link.

Steps **To Add a Conclusion and an Email Link**

1 **Scroll down the Instructions frame and then point to type a paragraph of text to serve as a conclusion (Figure 1-48).**

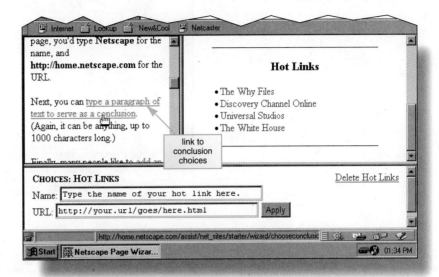

FIGURE 1-48

2 **Click type a paragraph of text. Drag through the text in the Conclusion text box to highlight it. Type (without pressing the ENTER key)** I hope you enjoyed visiting some of my favorite sites. Creating a Web page with the Page Wizard is much easier than writing HTML! **Point to the Apply button.**

As you type, the text displays in the Conclusion text box. You can scroll the text box to review what you typed (Figure 1-49).

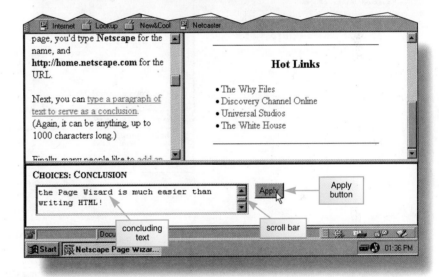

FIGURE 1-49

3 **Click the Apply button, and then scroll down the Preview frame to view the conclusion.**

After you click the Apply button, Page Wizard may take a moment to update the page in the Preview frame (Figure 1-50).

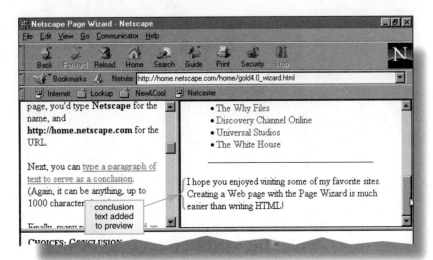

FIGURE 1-50

4 Scroll down the Instructions frame and then point to add an email link (Figure 1-51).

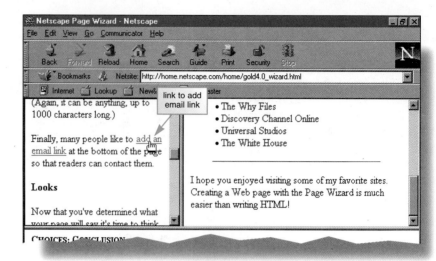

FIGURE 1-51

5 Click add an email link, and then highlight the text in the Email Link text box. Type jrobbins@email.myschool. edu **or your email address and then point to the Apply button.**

As you type, the text displays in the Email Link text box (Figure 1-52).

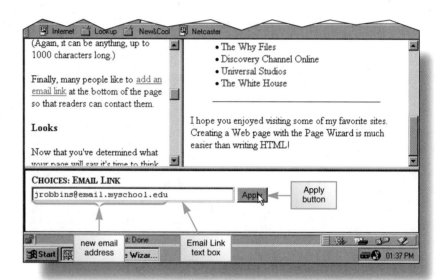

FIGURE 1-52

6 Click the Apply button. Scroll down the Preview frame to see your email hyperlink.

After you click the Apply button, it may take a moment for Page Wizard to update the page in the Preview frame (Figure 1-53).

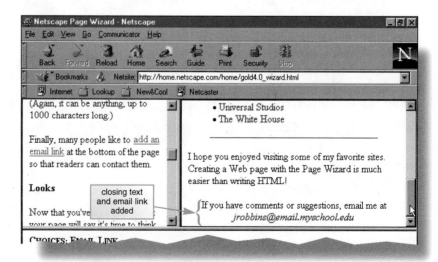

FIGURE 1-53

In the preceding steps, you supplied an email address to Page Wizard to create an email link on the page. Page Wizard automatically added some text preceding the email link, offering the reader an opportunity to send comments or suggestions. This is called the **signature** of the page.

More *About*
Page Appearance

Although color and images can enhance Web pages, you can find many pages where their use is overdone. For more information on Web page design guidelines, visit the Composer Web site (www.scsite.com/nc/pr1.htm) and click the link to Page Appearance.

Changing a Page's Appearance

Page Wizard offers several choices for enhancing the appearance of the page. You can choose from a set of color schemes, select your own custom colors, choose a texture for the page, choose from a set of bullet styles, and choose from a set of horizontal rules. Perform the following steps to add a color scheme, a bullet style, and a horizontal rule style.

 To Change a Page's Appearance

1 Scroll down the Instructions frame and then point to a preset color combination under Looks (Figure 1-54).

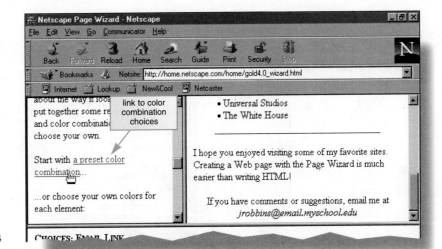

FIGURE 1-54

2 Click a preset color combination, and then point to a color combination of your choice in the Color Combination list.

John prefers the color combination pointed to in Figure 1-55.

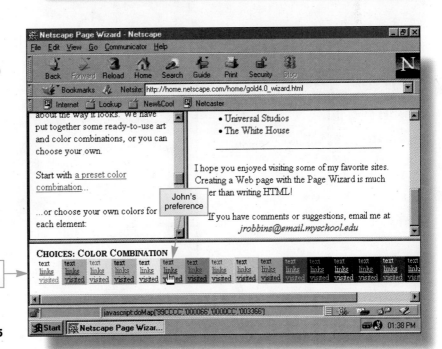

FIGURE 1-55

③ Click the color combination.

After you click the color combination, Page Wizard may take a moment to update the page in the Preview frame (Figure 1-56).

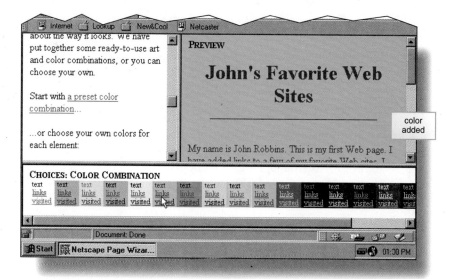

FIGURE 1-56

④ Scroll down the Instructions frame, and then point to choose a bullet style (Figure 1-57).

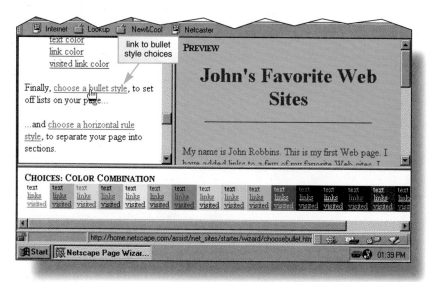

FIGURE 1-57

⑤ Click choose a bullet style. Point to one of the bullet styles in the Bullet Style list.

John prefers the bullet style pointed to in Figure 1-58.

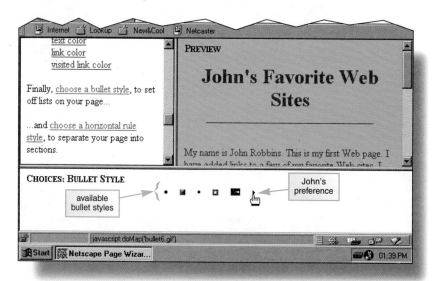

FIGURE 1-58

Netscape Composer

Creating a Web Page with Netscape's Page Wizard • NC 1.39

6 **Click a bullet style. Scroll down the Preview frame to see the updated bulleted list.**

After you click the desired bullet style, Page Wizard may take a moment to update the page in the Preview frame (Figure 1-59).

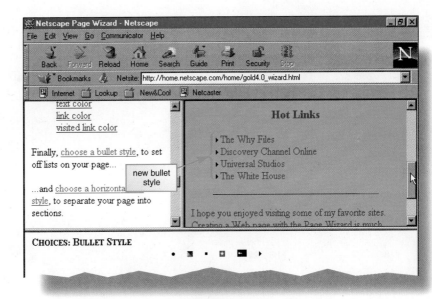

FIGURE 1-59

7 **Scroll down the Instructions frame, and then point to choose a horizontal rule style (Figure 1-60).**

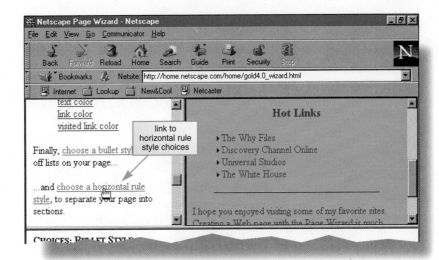

FIGURE 1-60

8 **Click choose a horizontal rule style, and then point to a style in the Horizontal Rule Style list.**

You can scroll the Choices frame to see additional horizontal rule styles. John prefers the one pointed to in Figure 1-61.

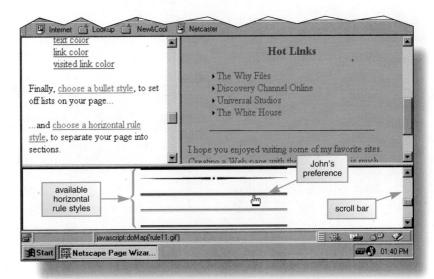

FIGURE 1-61

9 **Click a horizontal rule. Scroll down the Preview frame to see the new horizontal rules.**

After you click the horizontal rule, Page Wizard may take a moment to update the page in the Preview frame (Figure 1-62).

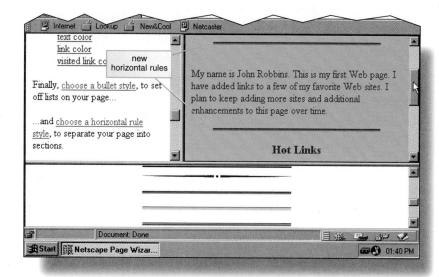

FIGURE 1-62

The discussion of HTML earlier in this project mentioned that you can have some variation in the appearance of bullets and horizontal rules through the use of keywords within the <UL> and <HR> tags. It is important to recognize that the bullets and horizontal rules added to the page in the preceding steps are not created with keywords, but are **inline images**.

Building and Saving a Page Wizard File

At this time, John's page exists only in the Preview frame of the Page Wizard. You can go back to the Instructions frame and click any of the features you want to change. Once you are satisfied with its appearance, the page must be built into an HTML file. Page Wizard will write the HTML file on Netscape's Web server, but then it must be saved locally. Otherwise, it would be deleted from Netscape's server after a period of time. Perform the following steps to build the HTML file and save it locally.

 Steps **To Build and Save a Page Wizard File**

1 **Scroll down to the bottom of the Instructions frame, and then point to the Build button.**

You would use the Start Over button to clear all entries you have made. The Build button builds the page when you click it (Figure 1-63).

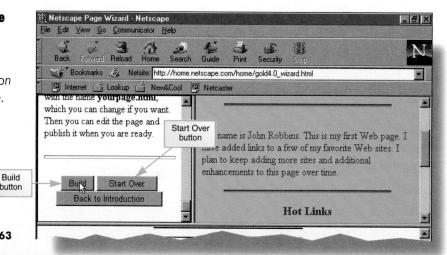

FIGURE 1-63

2 **Click the Build button.**

Page Wizard builds the HTML file and opens it in the Netscape browse window (Figure 1-64).

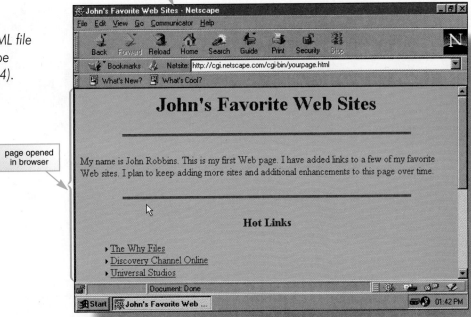

FIGURE 1-64

3 **Click File on the Navigator menu bar and then point to Edit Page.**

The File menu displays (Figure 1-65).

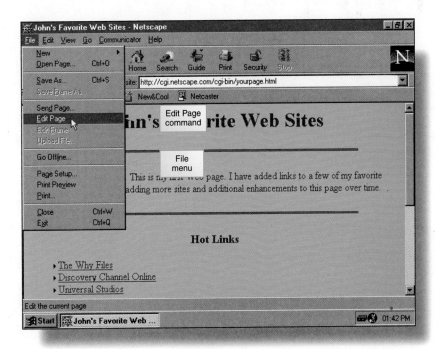

FIGURE 1-65

4 Click Edit Page.

The Composer window opens and the page displays (Figure 1-66). The page may display differently in the Composer window than in the Navigator window.

Netscape Composer window

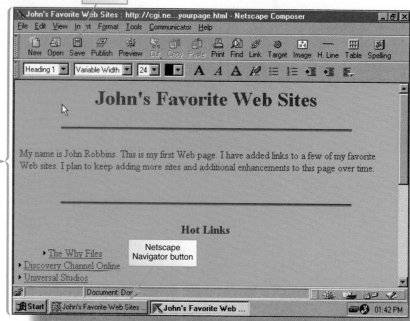

FIGURE 1-66

5 Click the Save button on the Composition toolbar.

The Save As dialog box displays (Figure 1-67).

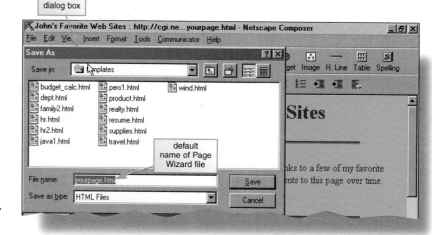

FIGURE 1-67

6 Type JohnsFavorite2 in the File name text box. Click the Save in box arrow and then click 3½ Floppy [A:].

The Save As dialog box displays as shown in Figure 1-68.

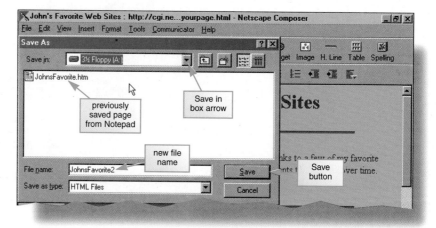

FIGURE 1-68

7 **Click the Save button in the Save As dialog box.**

Several files are saved on the floppy disk. Their names display in the Saving Page dialog box (Figure 1-69). The toolbars in the Composer window may be arranged differently on your screen. Composer may display the page differently than Navigator displays it.

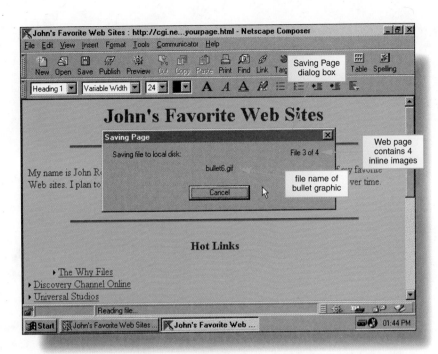

FIGURE 1-69

8 **Point to the Preview button on the Composition toolbar (Figure 1-70).**

The horizontal rules and bullets may appear differently in the Composer window than they did in the browse window (Figure 1-70)

FIGURE 1-70

9 Click the Preview button.

Netscape adds a browse window to the desktop and opens John's page in the browse window (Figure 1-71).

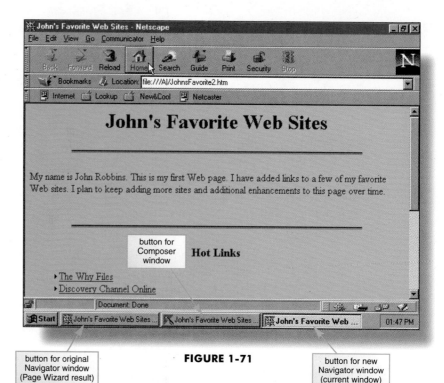

FIGURE 1-71

10 Test the remaining links on the page, and then scroll to the bottom of the page.

When Page Wizard built the page, it added a Netscape graphic as a hyperlink and some additional text (Figure 1-72).

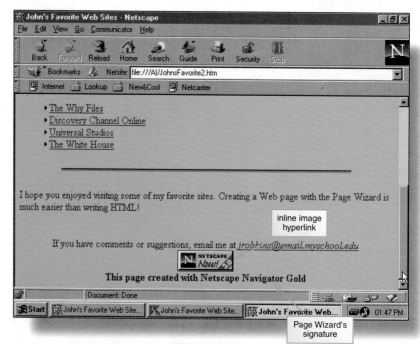

FIGURE 1-72

Other Ways

1. From Navigator window, press ALT+F, press E; from Composer window, press CTRL+S

In the preceding steps, you began the process of saving John's page locally by clicking Edit on the File menu. If you questioned why you did not click Save As on the File menu, the reason for this is that John's page contains inline images for the bullets and horizontal rules. Using Save As saves only the page itself, not the inline images. When you saved the page as you did in the preceding steps, all of the page's inline images also were saved locally.

Printing a Web Page from Composer

The Web page currently is displayed in a browse window. You can print the page from the browse window in the same way you previously have printed Web pages. You also can print a page from the Composer window at any time that Composer is open on the desktop. Perform the following steps to print John's Favorite Web Sites from Composer.

 Steps : **To Print a Web Page from Composer**

◆ **More** *About* **Printing Web Pages**

Web pages do not always display the same way in both the Navigator window and the Composer window. The page prints as it appears in the Navigator window whether you print it from Composer or Navigator. You can print the page directly from the Navigator window by clicking the Print button on the Navigation toolbar.

1 **Ready the printer. Click the Netscape Composer button on the taskbar and then point to the Print button on the Composition toolbar.**

The Composer window opens. The browse window can be accessed through its button on the taskbar (Figure 1-73).

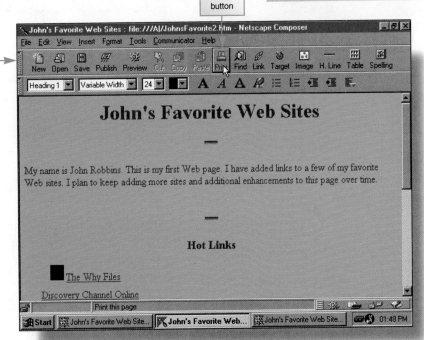

FIGURE 1-73

2 **Click the Print button.**

The Print dialog box displays (Figure 1-74).

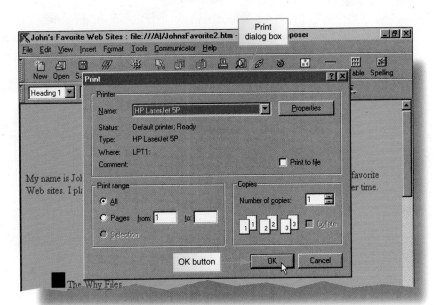

FIGURE 1-74

Click the OK button.

The page prints as shown in Figure 1-75.

| John's favorite Web Sites | file:///A|/JohnsFavorite2.htm |

John's Favorite Web Sites

My name is john Robbins. This is my first Web page. I have added links to some of my favorite Web sites. I plan to keep adding more sites and additional enhancements to this page over time.

Hot Links

- ▸ The Why Files
- ▸ Discovery Channel Online
- ▸ Universal Studios
- ▸ The White House

I hope you enjoyed visiting some of my favorite sites. Creating a Web page with the page Wizard is much easier than writing HTML!

If you have comments or suggestions, email me at jrobbins@email.myschool.edu

This page created with Netscape Navigator Gold

FIGURE 1-75

Some formatting features you add (such as word wrap around images) do not display in the Composer window, but do display when the page is viewed in the browser. When you print from Composer, however, the printout will be the same as it displays in the browse window.

Closing the Composer Window and Quitting Netscape

When you click Edit on the File menu in the Netscape Navigator window, the Netscape Composer window opens. When you click the Preview button on the Composition toolbar, the Netscape Composer window remains open and a new Navigator window opens in addition to any other Navigator windows already open. Perform the following steps to quit Netscape by closing the three windows.

TO CLOSE THE NAVIGATOR AND COMPOSER WINDOWS AND QUIT NETSCAPE

1. Click the Netscape Composer window Close button.
2. Click the Netscape Navigator (preview of JohnsFavorite) window Close button.
3. Click the Netscape Navigator (result of Page Wizard) window Close button.

Netscape closes.

Project Summary

Project 1 introduced you to HTML, Netscape Composer, and the Netscape Page Wizard. After learning the basics of HTML, you created a Web page by writing HTML code with a text editor. You saved the HTML file locally and viewed it with Netscape. You then created a Web page with similar content using the Netscape Page Wizard. You used Page Wizard to enhance the appearance of the second page. You then saved the page locally and viewed it with Netscape. You learned that although you have limited flexibility in page design and layout with the Page Wizard, you can accomplish these tasks more quickly and easily than writing HTML code yourself.

What You Should Know

Having completed this project, you now should be able to perform the following tasks:

- Add a Bulleted List and Links to Other Pages with HTML *(NC 1.20)*
- Add a Conclusion and an Email Link *(NC 1.35)*
- Add a Head Section and Title with HTML *(NC 1.17)*
- Add a Title, Heading, and Introduction *(NC 1.29)*
- Add Hot Links *(NC 1.32)*
- Add Italic Text and an Email Link with HTML *(NC 1.20)*
- Add Normal Text and Center a Heading with the ALIGN Keyword *(NC 1.19)*

- Begin the Body and Add a Centered Heading and Horizontal Rule with HTML *(NC 1.18)*
- Build and Save a Page Wizard File *(NC 1.40)*
- Change a Page's Appearance *(NC 1.37)*
- Close and Save an HTML File *(NC 1.21)*
- Close the Navigator and Composer Windows and Quit Netscape *(NC 1.46)*
- Open a New HTML File *(NC 1.17)*
- Print a Web Page from Composer *(NC 1.45)*
- Start Page Wizard *(NC 1.28)*
- View a Document's Source *(NC 1.13)*
- View and Test a Local HTML File in Netscape *(NC 1.24)*

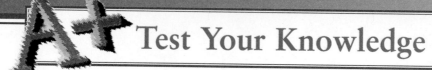

Test Your Knowledge

1 True/False

Instructions: Circle T if the statement is true or F if the statement is false.

T F   1. Rich Text Format (RTF) is the markup language used in Web pages.
T F   2. Inline images can be hyperlinks.
T F   3. Keywords always occur within tags.
T F   4. An HTML document's title should appear at the beginning of the body section.
T F   5. <LI> and </LI> are used to begin and end list items.
T F   6. Unordered list bullet types include circle, oval, and square.
T F   7. A link always takes you to another Web page.
T F   8. Page Wizard adds the title as a size 1 heading on the page.
T F   9. A page's texture is created by tiling a small image across the background.
T F 10. Page Wizard builds the HTML file as a local document.

2 Multiple Choice

Instructions: Circle the correct response.

1. A Web page created with a text editor is saved as which of the following file types?
   a. .doc
   b. .txt
   c. .htm
   d. .gif

2. Separate, independently scrolling areas within a browser are called _____.
   a. forms
   b. panels
   c. tables
   d. frames

3. Email links are created with the _____ keyword.
   a. SRC
   b. IMG
   c. HREF
   d. ALIGN

4. To save a remote document and its inline images locally, click _____ on the File menu.
   a. Edit
   b. View in Editor
   c. Document Source
   d. Save

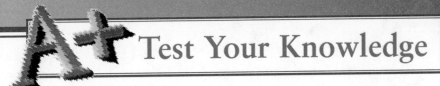

5. Page Wizard allows you to select an inline image for _____.
   a. bullets
   b. horizontal rules
   c. both a and b
   d. neither a nor b

6. An area of a Web page where the user enters information to be sent back to the server is called a
   _____.
   a. field
   b. frame
   c. pane
   d. form

7. Which of the following tags does not require an ending tag?
   a. <H1>
   b. <UL>
   c. <CENTER>
   d. none of the above

8. Word processor-like applications for creating Web pages are called _____.
   a. Web authoring tools
   b. HTML editors
   c. Web page editors
   d. all of the above

9. Transferring an HTML file and its associated files to a Web server for access by the entire World
   Wide Web is called _____ the page.
   a. publishing
   b. posting
   c. presenting
   d. previewing

10. Inline images _____ are located on the same server as the Web page.
   a. usually
   b. always
   c. never
   d. seldom

3 Understanding HTML

Instructions: Perform the following tasks using a computer.

1. Start Notepad
2. Open the JohnsFavorite file created with Notepad in Project 1.
3. Print the file.

(continued)

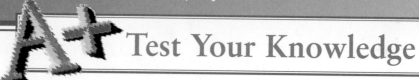

Understanding HTML *(continued)*

4. Open the JohnsFavorite2 file created by Page Wizard in Project 1.
5. Compare the two printouts. On JohnsFavorite2 printout, circle some of the tags that are not on the other printout.
6. Determine the functions of these tags (do not look them up in an HTML manual). *Hint*: You may want to view the page in the browser to help figure it out.
7. Write your name and your answers on the printout and hand it in to your instructor.

4 Editing HTML Documents

Instructions: Perform the following tasks using a computer.

1. Start Netscape.
2. Open the White House home page (www.whitehouse.gov).
3. Use View Page Source to find the HTML code for some feature that was not used on John's Favorite Web Sites page.
4. Highlight the code and copy it to the Clipboard (CTRL+C).
5. Open the file for John's page in Notepad.
6. Paste the Clipboard contents into John's page file.
7. Save John's revised page with the file name JohnsFavorite3.
8. Open JohnsFavorite3 in the browser.
9. Print the page. Write your name on the printout and hand it in to your instructor.

1 Netscape Authoring Guide

1. Start Netscape.
2. Click Help on the menu bar and then click Help Contents.
3. Click Composing and Editing Web Pages.
4. Read About Composer. Write down several things you can do with Composer that you cannot do with the Page Wizard.
5. Include your name with your answers and hand them in to your instructor.

2 Web Page Design Ideas

1. Start Netscape.
2. Click Help on the menu bar and then click Product Information and Support.
3. Scroll down the page to Other Useful Information and then click Web Page Starter.
4. Click the link to Gold Rush Contest Winners.
5. Scroll down to Honorable Mention Winners.
6. Under the Eureka Winners heading, view and print any five of the Web pages.
7. On the back of each page, write one thing about the page that appeals to you, one thing you did not like, and one idea the page gives you for creating your own pages.
8. Write your name on the pages and hand them in to your instructor.

1 Editing the Apply Your Knowledge Web Page

Instructions: Start Notepad. Open the file APPLY-1 from the folder specified by your instructor. Figure 1-76 shows the Apply Your Knowledge Web Page as it should appear in the Netscape browser. APPLY-1 is a partially completed HTML file (which also contains some errors) for this page. Perform the following tasks.

1. Open the file in Notepad.
2. Open the file in Netscape.
3. Examine the HTML file and its appearance in the browser.
4. Correct the HTML errors.
5. Add HTML code for the features shown in Figure 1-76 that currently are not included in the file.
6. Save the file, and name it APPLY-1A.
7. Print the revised document source.
8. Print the revised page as it appears in Netscape.
9. Write your name on the printouts and hand them in to your instructor.

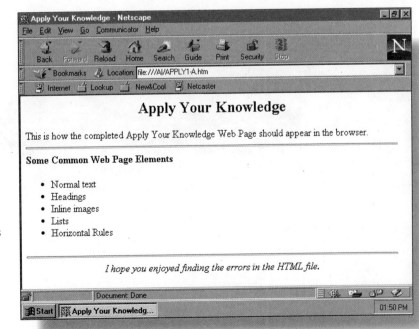

FIGURE 1-76

In the Lab

1 Class Schedule

Problem: Your instructor would like to make your class schedule available over the World Wide Web. You have been asked to create a Web page for the class schedule, similar to the one shown in Figure 1-77.

Instructions: Start Notepad and perform the following tasks.

1. Start a new HTML document with the title, [your name] LAB1-1 in the head section.
2. Begin the body section. Add a centered, size 1 heading that is the name of your class.
3. Add a horizontal rule.
4. Add a size 3 heading, Class Schedule.
5. Add a bulleted list of the dates and topics of class meetings.
6. Close the body, close the HTML document, and save the file, giving it the name LAB1-1.htm.
7. Open the LAB1-1.htm file in the Netscape browser.
8. Print the page and turn it in to your instructor.

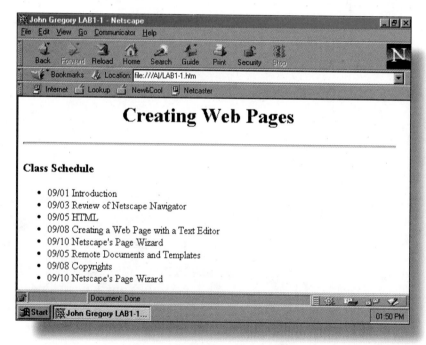

FIGURE 1-77

In the Lab

2 Web Search Engines

Problem: You want to create your own page of links to three of the search engines you use most that are available on the Web. Your completed page will be similar to the one shown in Figure 1-78.

Instructions: Obtain the URLs to any three of the Web search engines. Start Netscape and then perform the following tasks.

1. Start the Netscape Page Wizard.
2. Give the page the title, Web Search Engines
3. Add links to the three search engines you chose.
4. Select any preset color combination.
5. Select any bullet style and horizontal rule style.
6. Build the page.
7. Open the page in a Composer window and then save the page locally with the file name LAB1-2.
8. Right-click the horizontal rule above Hot Links and then click Cut on the shortcut menu.
9. View and test the page in the browser and then print it.
10. Write your name on the printout and turn it in to your instructor.

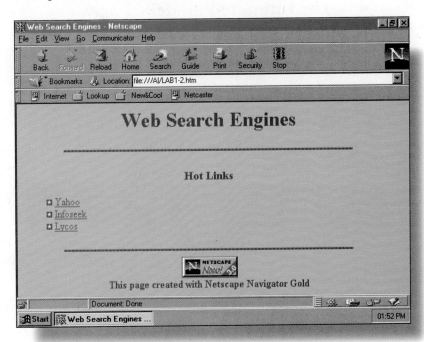

FIGURE 1-78

In the Lab

3 Starting a Home Page

Problem: You want to create a home page for your favorite sport or hobby. Realizing that good pages develo over time and constantly are being revised, you want to start now.

Instructions: Start Notepad and perform the following tasks.

1. Create a Web page about one of your interests, similar to the one shown in Figure 1-79.
2. The page title should be [your name] LAB1-3.
3. Include an email link (you can make one up if you do not have one).
4. Save the page with the file name LAB1-3.htm.
5. Print the page from the Netscape browser and turn in the printout to your instructor.

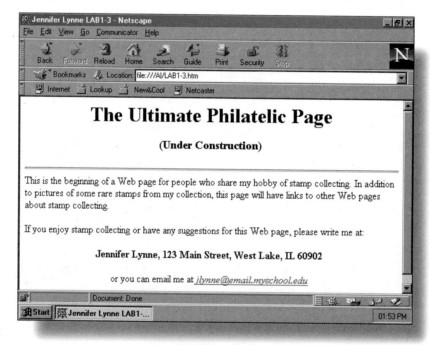

FIGURE 1-79

Cases and Places

The difficulty of these case studies varies: ❿ are the least difficult; ❿❿ are more difficult; and ❿❿❿ are the most difficult.

1 ❿ John is not satisfied with the page you created for him in Project 1. He feels it is bland and would like you to put some life into it. Rebuild John's Favorite Web Sites using Netscape's Page Wizard. Take advantage of any of Page Wizard's features (such as custom colors) that you think will add interest to the page.

2 ❿ Your instructor wants to make his course syllabus available over the Web. Use Notepad to create a text-only course home page for your class that includes information from the syllabus.

3 ❿❿ Many theme parks have a booth where you can have your picture taken and then pasted into the cover of a well-known magazine. An entrepreneur friend thinks a commercially viable equivalent may exist on the Web. He has asked you to work with him. Save any prominent Web page locally and then edit its source to insert the name and some personal information about yourself or a friend.

4 ❿❿ You want to create your own Favorite Web Sites page. You do not want to write all the HTML code. You like the Page Wizard's basic layout, but you want features Page Wizard cannot offer (a numbered list, five links to other pages, the heading, Top Five, instead of Hot Links, and more). Create your own Favorite Web Sites page. Start by building as much of the page as you can with Page Wizard and then use Notepad to add additional features.

5 ❿❿❿ The instructor in one of your classes is impressed with a report you wrote. She wants you to make the paper available over the Web as a model to other students. Take any report or paper you have written with a word processor and export the document as a plain text file (most word processors will do this). Edit the text file to make it an HTML document.

6 ❿❿❿ The HyperText Markup Language (HTML) contains many more tags than those presented in this project. It is evolving continuously and additional tags are added to each new version. Find some sources of information about HTML on the Web. Learn about some tags not presented in this project. Build a Web page that includes those tags.

Cases and Places

7 ▶▶▶ You often will find Web pages that are lists of links to other pages on a particular subject. Whether you are browsing the Web casually or searching seriously for information, this type of Web page is very valuable. Many of these pages have been created by individuals such as yourself, who have some particular interest, have searched the Web for information on that area of interest, and want to share what they have found. Select any topic of interest to you. Search the Web for pages related to that topic. Create a Web page that provides a list of links to the pages you found with a brief description of each page.

Netscape Composer

Creating Web Pages from Templates and Remote Documents

Objectives:

You will have mastered the material in this project when you can:

- ▶ Define remote and local documents
- ▶ Explain the purpose of templates
- ▶ List major copyright concerns
- ▶ Explain the function of targets
- ▶ Set Composer preferences
- ▶ Arrange the toolbars
- ▶ Open a remote template file
- ▶ Remove links
- ▶ Add and delete text
- ▶ Find and replace text
- ▶ Set character properties
- ▶ Set paragraph properties
- ▶ Create lists
- ▶ Insert horizontal rules
- ▶ Add targets and links to targets
- ▶ Save and view a template document

Project 2

Information Riches on the Electronic *Silk Road*

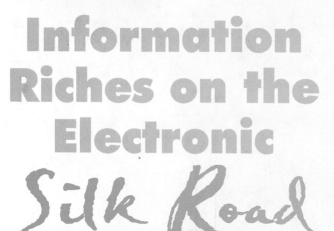

Traveling from one exciting Internet site to the next can make you feel like a merchant-explorer in a new online world. Every site leads to countless new ones, all brimming with the riches of information, ideas, knowledge, and news. Most exciting of all is the part of the Internet called the World Wide Web (WWW), which stores thousands of hypermedia documents and provides a new route for communication and commerce.

The World Wide Web links today's world: high-powered telephone lines connect thousands of servers around the globe, each containing pages of information. Long before the birth of the Web, the Silk Road connected the world. For 2,000 years, this road — a tenuous thread of communication and commerce that stretched from China to Europe — was a highway for caravans of merchants laden with silk, gold, and glass, trading goods and sharing culture along the way. Like the Web, the Silk Road was not merely a single route, it had many different branches that connected different towns.

merchant-explorer in a new online world

Tim Berners-Lee, the father of the Web, was the first to travel the hyperlinks of the Web. While working at CERN, the European Particle Physics Laboratory in Switzerland in the 1980s, Berners-Lee wrote a program called Enquire, which stored information using random associations and used hypertext to move around the Internet. In 1989, Berners-Lee proposed the Web, and travel on the Web was underway.

Today, all you need is a modem, an Internet service provider, and a Web browser, and you are ready to explore this electronic Silk Road. Your Web browser is your golden tablet, providing passage between linked sites all over the world.

Browsing the World Wide Web is the Silk Road to learning essential Web page design. Looking at other's work, you quickly can recognize good and bad practices. For sources of ideas, visit sites that have received design awards or have won design competition such as the Netscape Gold Rush Contest.

In this project, you will create Web pages from a remote template in Composer. The template is an existing HTML file that has been organized and formatted with a basic framework of content. When you connect to the Netscape Template Web site, you select a category, and then you are presented with step-by-step instructions that guide you through basic Composer features, where you provide information to personalize your page. The Netscape Template Web site is located on the Netscape home site, which you access via your connection to the Internet

Like the Silk Road, you can experience the wealth of the Web. In your Web travels, you can gather the richness of ideas, insight, and design that only browsing the Web can provide.

```html
<!DOCTYPE HTML PUBLIC "-//W3C//
<HTML>
<HEAD>
    <TITLE>Tim  Berners-Lee</TITLE>
    </HEAD>
    <BODY BGCOLOR="#ffffff">
    <P>
<IMG  SRC="tim.gif"      HEIGHT=103  WIDTH=
<LI>
    If  you  need  someone  to  find  something
    (travel    agents,    or  parakeets    or  whatev
    <A  HREF="/pub/DataSources/bySubject/Overview.htr
for   example.
<LI>
    If  you  want  to  know  how  to  run  a  server,
        <A  HREF="/">W3C  web</A>  or  your  local  books
<LI>
    For  bug  reports    on  the  cern-httpd    server,    ma
    <A  HREF="mailto:httpd@w3.org">httpd@w3.org</A>
<LI>
    If  you  can't    access  something    on  <TT>www.w3.org</T
    <A  HREF="mailto:webmaster@w3.org">webmaster@w3.org</A>
    found  the  bad  link  not  just  where  it  went  to.
<LI>
    If  you  find  bad  links  from  www.w3.org  pages  or  errors
    please    mail  <A  HREF="webmaster@w3.org">webmaster@w3.org</A
<LI>
<A  HREF="../../Talks/">Slides
<LI>
<A  HREF="Mainspring.html">Disclosure:
    </UL>
    <UL>
<A  HREF="9602affi.html">Presentation    to  CDA  challenge  by  CDT  e
    </UL>
    <UL>
    <LI>
<A  HREF="951217-NYT/">Article    in  NY  Times  Dec  18  1995</A>
    </UL>
```

Project 2

Netscape Composer

Case Perspective

Mary Cunningham is financing her school tuition by running a small catering service. A local business association provides free space on its Web server and a link from its home page to local businesses such as hers. Qualifying businesses, however, must create and maintain their own Web pages. Mary has asked you to help.

You may recall that it was Mary who first told you about the Netscape Page Wizard. Mary has some ideas about the design of her catering business page. She realizes what she wants is beyond the capabilities of the Page Wizard. Mary would like the page to have a bulleted list of links to the major topic areas within the page, some pictures, and an appropriate use of color to enhance the text and background. Rather than create Mary's page from scratch, you have decided to use some of the basic features of Netscape Composer to create Mary's page by modifying a Web page template.

Creating Web Pages from Templates and Remote Documents

Introduction

Browsing the World Wide Web is a good way to begin learning Web page design. You can identify some good and bad practices quickly just by looking at what other people have done. Sites that have received design awards or have won design competitions such as the Netscape Gold Rush Contest are good sources of ideas for designing your own pages.

You know from your previous use of Netscape that you can make a local copy of any image you see on a Web page by right-clicking the image. You learned in Project 1 how to *get inside* a Web page by viewing its HTML source and copying and pasting any part you want into your own document.

So, why re-invent the wheel when you are constructing your own pages? Why not take the best of what you see and modify, cut, and paste to fit your needs? This can be an efficient way to develop well-designed pages under certain circumstances. If the material you are copying or modifying is copyrighted, however, you may be breaking the law.

What Are Remote Documents and Templates?

A **remote document** is any Web page that resides on a Web server somewhere on the Internet that you view through the Netscape browser. In this project, you will create the Cunningham Catering Web page (Figure 2-1 and Figure 2-2 on pages NC 2.5 and NC 2.6) by modifying a Web page template. A **Web page template** is an HTML file that has been organized and formatted with a basic framework of content for you to modify to fit your needs. The closer the template is to the design you are looking for, the less work you have to do. **Consistency** is an important design characteristic for Web sites that are composed of multiple pages. This means the pages are similar in their use of features, such as background color, margins, horizontal rules, and sizes of headings. Templates are useful especially for maintaining consistency when building a multipage Web site.

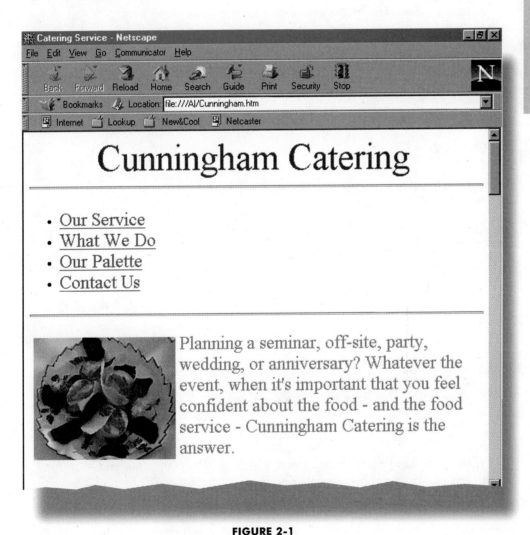

FIGURE 2-1

More *About* **Templates**

By modifying Web page templates that are available for you to use, you can save a lot of time and create some very powerful Web pages. For more sources of Web page templates, visit the Composer Web site (www.scsite.com/nc/pr2.htm) and click the link to More Templates.

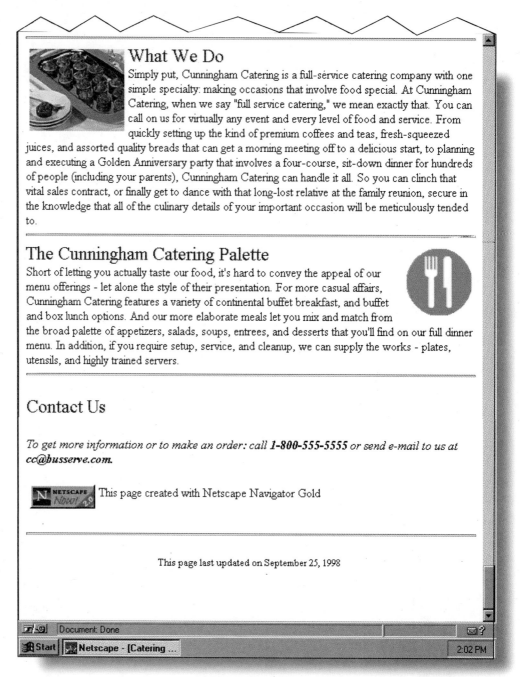

FIGURE 2-2

A template can be a **local document**, which is a file you create and keep for your own use, or it can be a **remote document**, such as the set of templates on the Netscape Communications Corporation's Web server. These templates are made available to anyone on the Web and can be accessed through the Netscape browser's File menu. At this point, you might be questioning, Why not save any remote document locally and then use it as a template? The answer is, you can, but being able to do it does not mean you have permission to do it.

Copyrights

Suppose you invested a great amount of energy creating a Web page for your small business, which included some original artwork and images scanned from photographs you took. How would you feel if you were surfing the Web one day and found a copy of your page with only the slightest modifications, such as someone else's name on it? Would you be flattered or angry? Would it make a difference if the copy were used for someone else's home page or a business that competes with yours?

The underlying design of a Web page consists of an arrangement of elements such as text, images, audio, and video. As long as that design is original and nontrivial, it can be protected by copyright. Many Web pages have a copyright statement near the bottom of the page. It is permissible to use copyrighted material under certain circumstances called the **fair use limitation on exclusive rights**. The safest way to protect yourself from copyright violation, however, is to get permission to use any copyrighted images or documents.

In this project, you will modify one of the Netscape Web Page Templates. Users of Netscape Composer have permission from Netscape Communications Corporation to modify and reuse the Netscape Web Page Templates.

More *About*
Fair Use

Several tests exist that can help you determine if the Fair Use Limitation applies to your situation. For more information on the Fair Use Limitation, visit the Composer Web site (www.scsite.com/nc/pr2.htm) and click the link to Fair Use.

Project Two – Cunningham Catering

After talking with Mary about her ideas, you searched several sources of Web page templates and found one that seemed a good candidate for Mary's page. In a second meeting, you and Mary reviewed the template and identified the changes that need to be made (Figure 2-3 on the next page).

The template you have decided to use comes from Netscape Communications Corporation, and you have checked to make sure no restrictions apply on its use. Using Netscape Composer, you will save the template locally and make the necessary changes.

Project Steps

The following tasks will be completed in this project.

1. Open a Netscape browse window.
2. Set Composer preferences.
3. Open an Composer window.
4. Arrange the toolbars.
5. Open a remote template in an edit window.
6. Edit text.
7. Set character and paragraph properties.
8. Add a bullet list and horizontal line.
9. Insert linked targets.
10. Save and test the page.

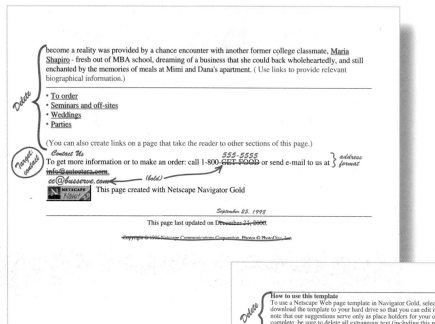

Delete ⟨ become a reality was provided by a chance encounter with another former college classmate, <u>Maria Shapiro</u> - fresh out of MBA school, dreaming of a business that she could back wholeheartedly, and still enchanted by the memories of meals at Mimi and Dana's apartment. (Use links to provide relevant biographical information.)

- <u>To order</u>
- <u>Seminars and off-sites</u>
- <u>Weddings</u>
- <u>Parties</u>

(You can also create links on a page that take the reader to other sections of this page.)

Target! contact

Contact Us

To get more information or to make an order: call 1-800-~~GET FOOD~~ *555-5555* or send e-mail to us at } *address format*

~~info@eatcetera.com.~~

cc@busserve.com ← *(bold)*

This page created with Netscape Navigator Gold

September 25, 1998

This page last updated on ~~December 21, 2000.~~

~~Copyright © 1996 Netscape Communications Corporation. Photos © PhotoDisc, Inc.~~

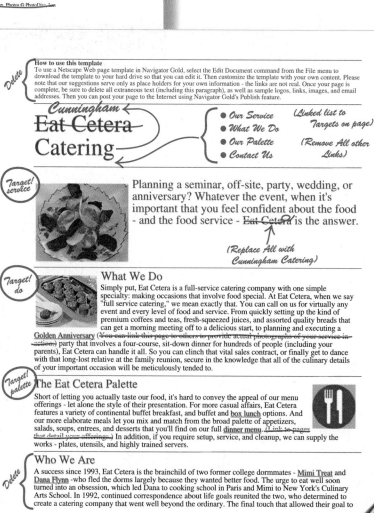

Delete ⟨ **How to use this template**
To use a Netscape Web page template in Navigator Gold, select the Edit Document command from the File menu to download the template to your hard drive so that you can edit it. Then customize the template with your own content. Please note that our suggestions serve only as place holders for your own information - the links are not real. Once your page is complete, be sure to delete all extraneous text (including this paragraph), as well as sample logos, links, images, and email addresses. Then you can post your page to the Internet using Navigator Gold's Publish feature.

Cunningham ←

Eat Cetera Catering ⟩

- Our Service
- What We Do
- Our Palette
- Contact Us

(Linked list to Targets on page)

(Remove All other Links)

Target! service

Planning a seminar, off-site, party, wedding, or anniversary? Whatever the event, when it's important that you feel confident about the food - and the food service - ~~Eat Cetera~~ is the answer.

(Replace All with Cunningham Catering)

Target! do

What We Do

Simply put, Eat Cetera is a full-service catering company with one simple specialty: making occasions that involve food special. At Eat Cetera, when we say "full service catering," we mean exactly that. You can call on us for virtually any event and every level of food and service. From quickly setting up the kind of premium coffees and teas, fresh-squeezed juices, and assorted quality breads that can get a morning meeting off to a delicious start, to planning and executing a <u>Golden Anniversary</u> ~~(You can link this page to others to provide actual photographs of your service in action.)~~ party that involves a four-course, sit-down dinner for hundreds of people (including your parents), Eat Cetera can handle it all. So you can clinch that vital sales contract, or finally get to dance with that long-lost relative at the family reunion, secure in the knowledge that all of the culinary details of your important occasion will be meticulously tended to.

Target! palette

The Eat Cetera Palette

Short of letting you actually taste our food, it's hard to convey the appeal of our menu offerings - let alone the style of their presentation. For more casual affairs, Eat Cetera features a variety of continental buffet breakfast, and buffet and <u>box lunch</u> options. And our more elaborate meals let you mix and match from the broad palette of appetizers, salads, soups, entrees, and desserts that you'll find on our full <u>dinner menu</u>. ~~(Link to pages that detail your offerings.)~~ In addition, if you require setup, service, and cleanup, we can supply the works - plates, utensils, and highly trained servers.

Delete ⟨ ## Who We Are

A success since 1993, Eat Cetera is the brainchild of two former college dormmates - <u>Mimi Treat</u> and <u>Dana Flynn</u> -who fled the dorms largely because they wanted better food. The urge to eat well soon turned into an obsession, which led Dana to cooking school in Paris and Mimi to New York's Culinary Arts School. In 1992, continued correspondence about life goals reunited the two, who determined to create a catering company that went well beyond the ordinary. The final touch that allowed their goal to

FIGURE 2-3

Setting Composer Preferences, Starting Composer, and Working with Composer Toolbars

When you first start Netscape Communicator, a Navigator **browse window** (Figure 2-4) displays. This is the window you are accustomed to working with when you browse the Web. Documents are created or modified in a different window, the **Composer window**, shown in Figure 2-5. Each document you are creating or editing has its own window and you can have multiple Composer windows open at the same time, just as you can have multiple browse windows open at the same time. You can set **Composer preferences** that affect various properties of all of the documents you work with in any Composer window.

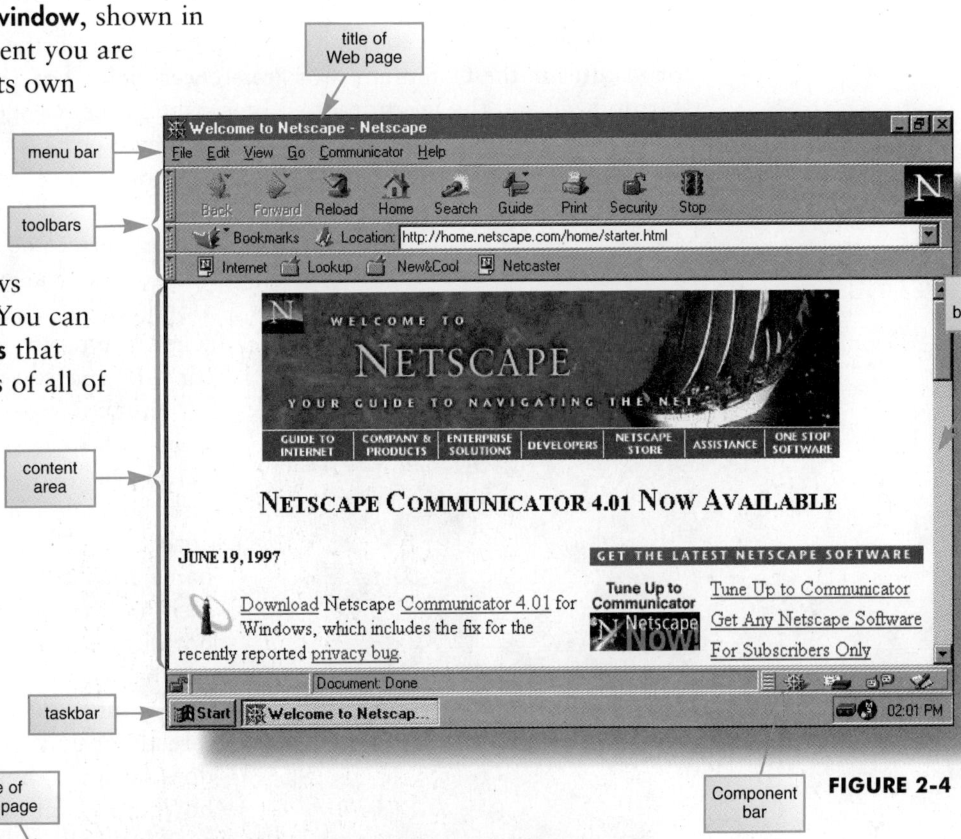

FIGURE 2-4

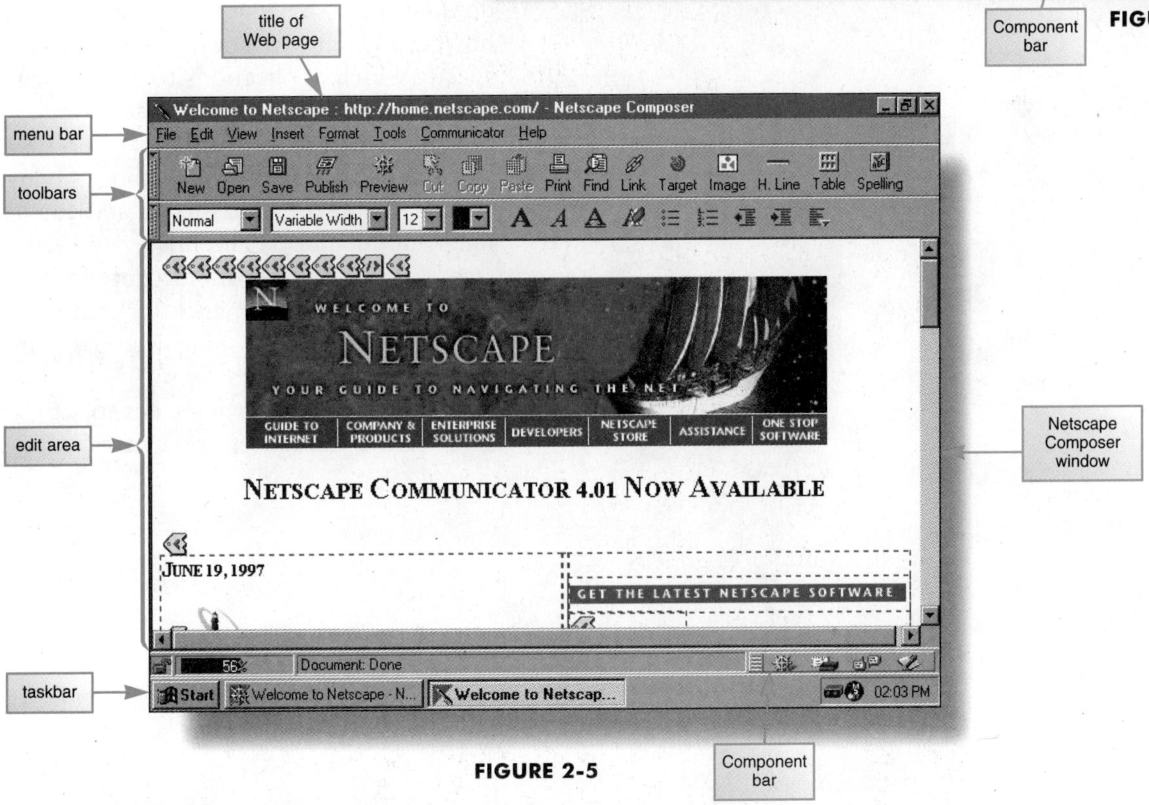

FIGURE 2-5

Two toolbars are available for your use in the Composer window, and you have several options for setting the display and locations of these toolbars. A Composer window can be opened in any one of several ways, depending on the location of the document you want to create or edit. In the steps that follow, you will set some of the Composer preferences, open a Composer window and arrange the toolbars.

Setting Composer Preferences

You can set default values for several categories of the Netscape Communicator features in the Communicator **Preferences dialog box** (Figure 2-6). You set the startup page and the location of a home page in the **Navigator category**. You can set the type of toolbar buttons for all Communicator applications (including Navigator and Composer) in the **Appearance category** (Figure 2-7). In this category, you also specify which of Communicator's components will start when you double-click the Communicator shortcut icon on the desktop.

In the **Composer category**, you can indicate how frequently you want the current page to be saved automatically and the name you want to display as the author of the document. The author's name entered here displays in the head section of the HTML document but does not display when the document is viewed in a browse window. Sometimes, you may want to edit the HTML source code directly or edit an image file. Composer does not provide facilities for either; however, Composer does allow you to specify which applications to open when you want to edit HTML source code directly or edit image files.

You can specify features about saving remote documents and images and copying local documents and images to Web servers in the Publish subcategory in the Composer category (Figure 2-7). You will learn about publishing Web pages in Project 3.

Perform the following steps to set some of the Composer preferences.

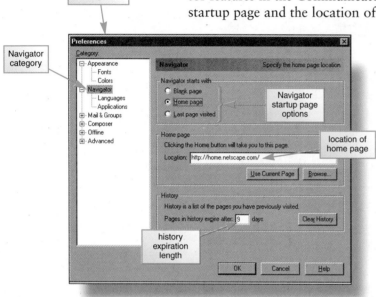

FIGURE 2-6

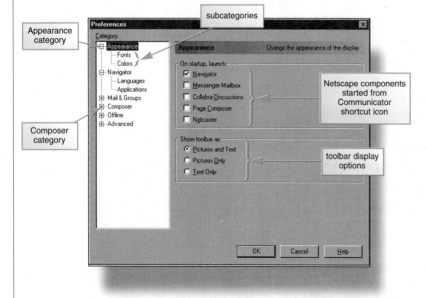

FIGURE 2-7

Steps **To Set Composer Preferences**

title of page
displays

1 **Double-click the Netscape
Communicator shortcut icon on
the desktop. Click Edit on the
menu bar and then point to
Preferences.**

*Netscape Communicator starts and
opens a Navigator window. The Edit
menu displays (Figure 2-8). Your
browser may display a different
startup page.*

startup
page

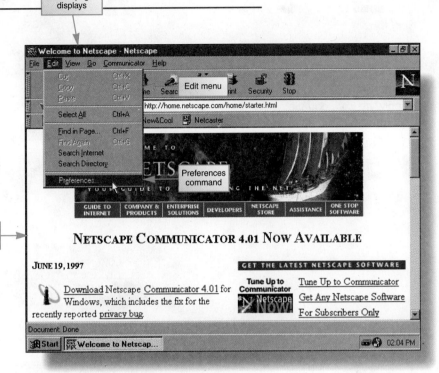

FIGURE 2-8

2 **Click Preferences and then point
to Composer in the Category tree
list.**

*The Preferences dialog box displays
(Figure 2-9).*

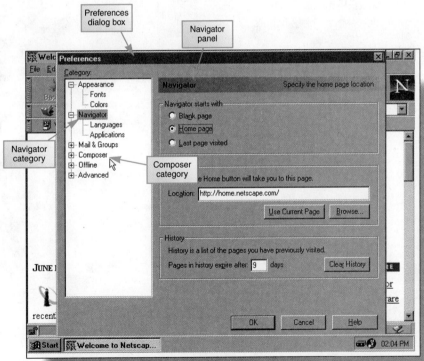

FIGURE 2-9

3 Click Composer and then type your name in the Author Name text box.

If you have separate applications on your PC to use for editing HTML source code or image files, you can supply the path and file name of the application in the text boxes in the External Editors area (Figure 2-10).

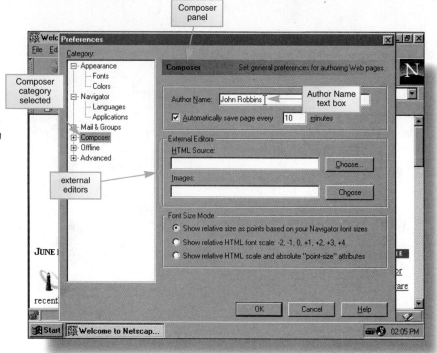

FIGURE 2-10

4 Double-click Composer and then point to Publishing.

The tree list expands to show the Publishing subcategory (Figure 2-11).

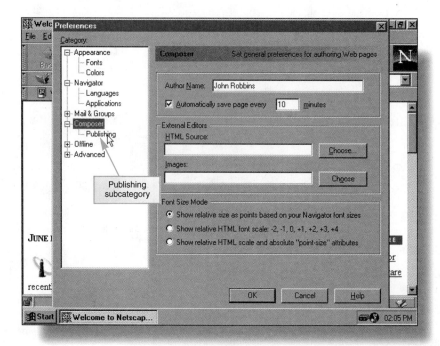

FIGURE 2-11

5 Click Publishing.

The Publishing panel displays (Figure 2-12).

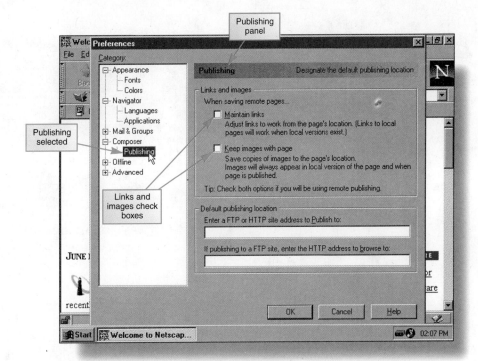

FIGURE 2-12

6 If check marks are not present, click both of the Links and images check boxes. Point to the OK button.

These options should be selected to maintain links and save copies of the images within the templates you will use (Figure 2-13).

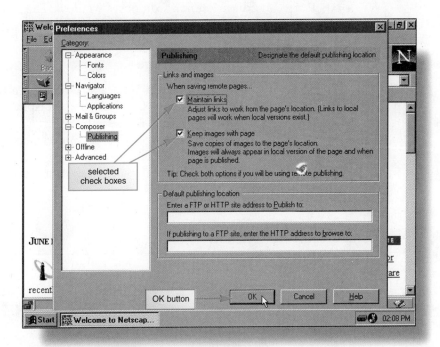

FIGURE 2-13

7 **Click the OK button.**

The Preferences dialog box closes (Figure 2-14).

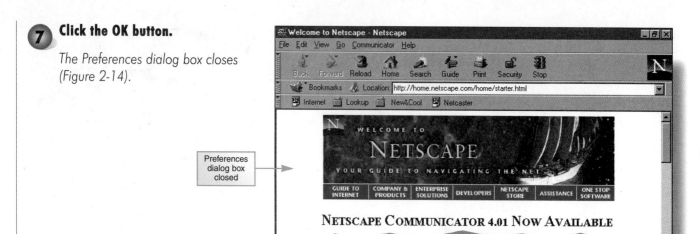

Preferences dialog box closed

FIGURE 2-14

Both the Navigator window and the Composer window contain Edit menus. In the preceding steps, you opened the Preferences dialog box from the Edit menu of the Navigator window. You also can open the Preferences dialog box from the Edit menu in a Composer window. The last command on the Edit menu is Preferences in both the Navigator and Composer windows.

Starting Netscape Composer

When you start Netscape Communicator, a browse window opens and the home page specified in Preferences displays. Several ways to open a Composer window from the browse window are possible, depending on the task you want to perform. You opened a Composer window in Project 1 by clicking Edit on the browse window's File menu.

Perform the following steps to use the Component bar to open a Composer window.

Steps **To Open a Composer Window**

1 **Point to the Composer icon on the Component bar (Figure 2-15).**

You can also start Navigator, Mail, and Discussion windows from the Component bar.

FIGURE 2-15

Component bar

Composer icon

2 Click the Composer icon.

Netscape opens a new Composer window in addition to the Navigator window (Figure 2-16).

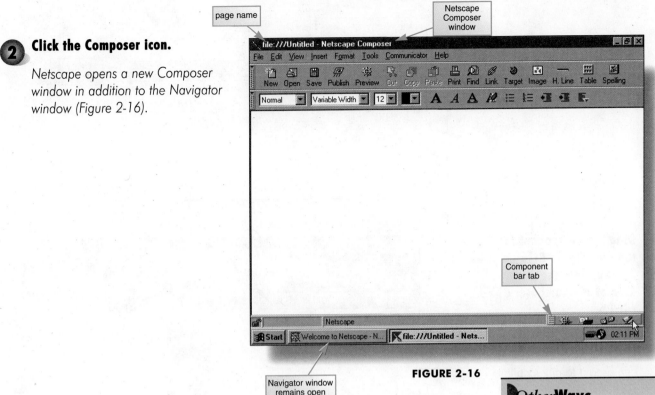

FIGURE 2-16

Other Ways

1. Click Start button on taskbar, point to Programs, point to Netscape Communicator, click Netscape Composer

When a Composer window is opened, it does not replace the browse window. The browse window remains open on the desktop.

Working with the Composer Toolbars

Netscape Composer has two toolbars that contain buttons that serve as short-cuts to many of the editing features available through Composer menus. The **Composition toolbar** (Figure 2-17) contains buttons to create, open, and save Web pages; perform editing functions; create links and targets; insert images, horizontal rules, and tables; check spelling; preview your Web page in the browser; and publish pages on a remote server.

You will use the **Formatting toolbar** (Figure 2-18) to apply paragraph format-ting; set font styles, sizes, and colors; and set text indenting and alignment.

You can hide or display these toolbars and you can change their arrangement at the top of the Composer window. You also can drag the Component bar on top of the Composer window or you can dock it at the lower-right corner of the window. Perform the steps on the next page to arrange the toolbars.

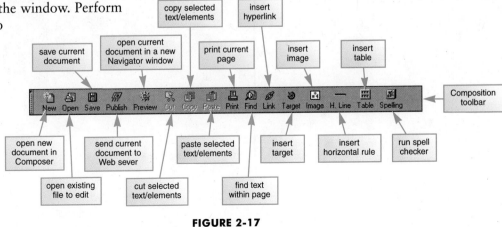

FIGURE 2-17

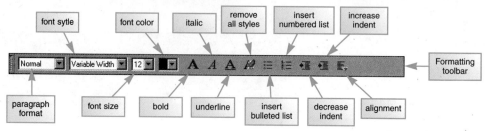

FIGURE 2-18

Steps **To Arrange the Toolbars**

1 **Drag the Component toolbar tab (see Figure 2-16 on page NC 2.15) up into the edit area of the Composer window.**

The Component bar floats on top of the window and you can drag it to any location on the desktop (Figure 2-19).

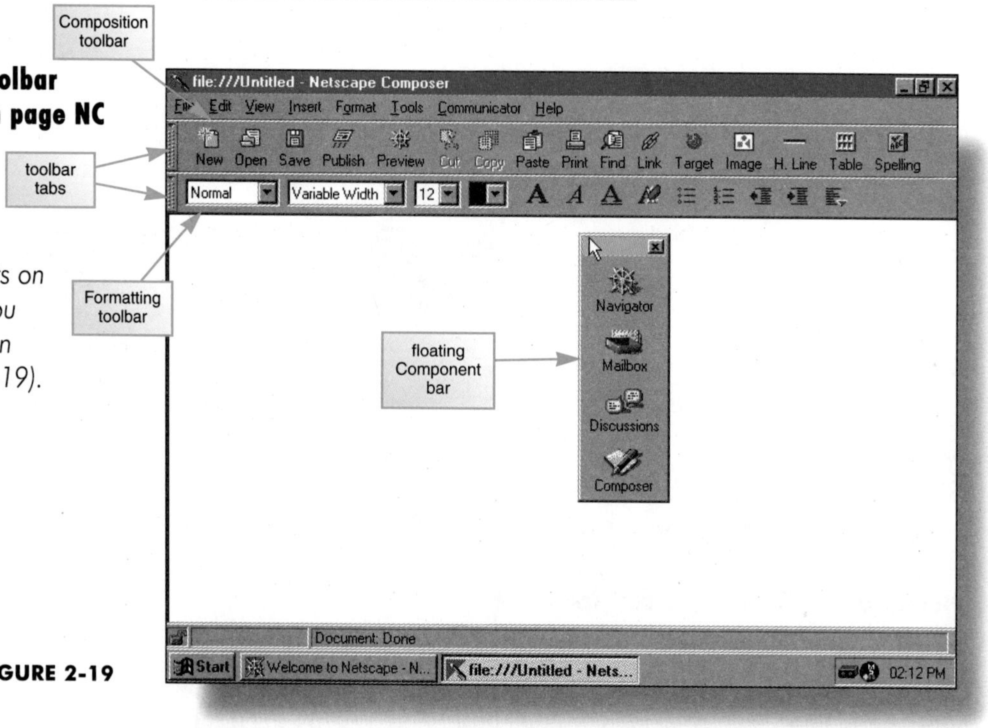

FIGURE 2-19

2 **Click the Formatting toolbar tab and then click the Composition toolbar tab.**

The toolbars close (Figure 2-20).

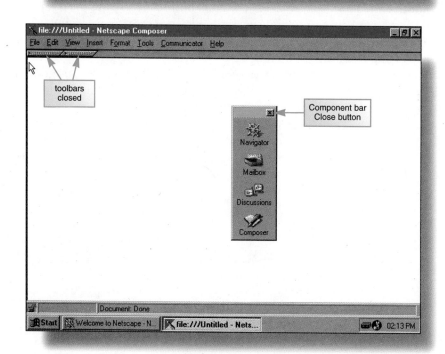

FIGURE 2-20

3 Click the Component bar Close button.

The Component bar docks at the bottom of the window (Figure 2-21).

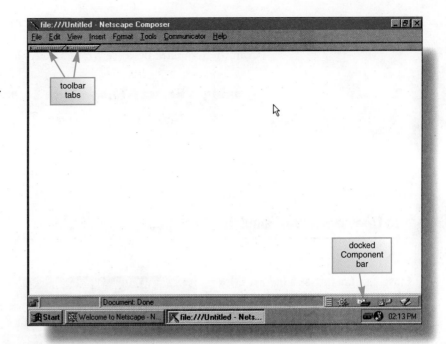

FIGURE 2-21

4 Click the Formatting toolbar tab and then click the Composition toolbar tab.

The toolbars display as shown in Figure 2-22.

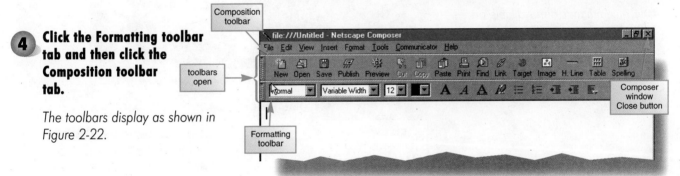

FIGURE 2-22

Other Ways
1. On View menu click Hide or Show for appropriate tool-bar

As you can see from the preceding steps, you can make many possible toolbar arrangements. If the Formatting toolbar is above the Composition toolbar, drag the Composition toolbar tab downward. This will switch the locations of the toolbars so they display as shown in Figure 2-22.

Opening a Template in Composer and Removing Links

When you open a template from either a Navigator or a Composer window, an additional browse (Navigator) window is opened containing whichever page you specified as the Template Location in the New Page From Template dialog box.

You can open any remote location for a template or you can open the Netscape Web Page Templates page. This page contains links to several pages, which are templates for you to use. In addition to the links to template pages, the Web Page Templates page contains links to some very good sources of information about copyrights.

Netscape template pages contain fictitious links to suggest to you places on the page where you might add your own links. You will remove all of the links from the template because Mary's page does not include links to other pages.

Opening a Remote Template in Composer

To use a Netscape Web page template, first you must download the template to a local drive so you can save changes you make to the page. Perform the following steps to open the Netscape Web Page Templates page, open the Eat Cetera Catering template, and save it on a floppy disk in drive A.

 Steps To Open a Remote Template in Composer

1 **Close the Composer window. Click File on the menu bar, point to New, and point to Page From Template.**

Five commands are available on the New submenu (Figure 2-23).

New command

File menu

New submenu

Page From Template command

Composer window closed

FIGURE 2-23

2 Click Page From Template and then point to the Netscape Templates button.

You can enter a URL, display a File Open dialog box, or go to the Netscape Templates Page from the New Page From Template dialog box (Figure 2-24). (The template for this project also is available at www.scsite.com/nc/pr2.htm.)

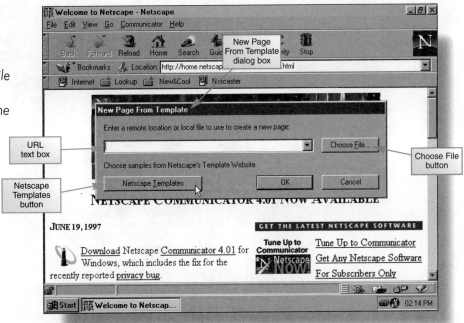

FIGURE 2-24

3 Click the Netscape Templates button. Scroll down the page to template categories.

A second Navigator window is opened with the Netscape Templates Page. The Netscape templates are grouped by categories (Figure 2-25).

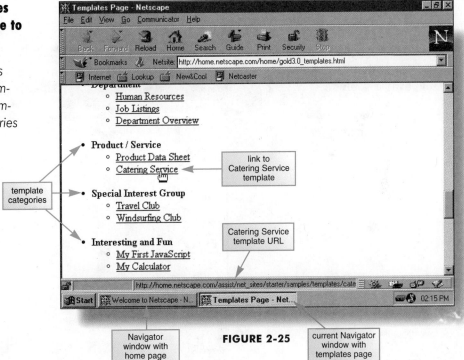

FIGURE 2-25

4 **Click Catering Service, click File on the menu bar, and then point to Edit Page.**

The Eat Cetera Catering template is opened in the second browse window (Figure 2-26).

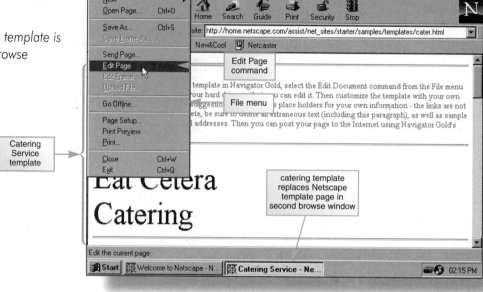

FIGURE 2-26

5 **Click Edit Page and then point to the Save button on the Composition toolbar.**

A Composer window opens with the Eat Cetera template (Figure 2-27).

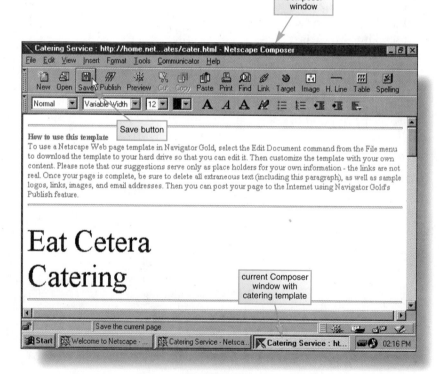

FIGURE 2-27

6 Click the Save button. Insert a floppy disk in drive A. Type `Cunningham` in the File name text box, click 3½ Floppy [A:] in the Save in list box, and click the Save button in the Save As dialog box. Close the two browse windows.

The Eat Cetera Catering page is saved as a local document on the floppy disk in drive A and the page displays in the edit area of the Composer window (Figure 2-28).

page name

file name

Navigator window with home page closed

Navigator window with catering template closed

FIGURE 2-28

Other Ways

1. From Composer window, click New button on Composition toolbar, click From Template button

When you saved the Eat Cetera Catering page in the previous steps, Composer automatically saved all of the inline images within the document as local files also. If you previously had saved any of the inline images, Composer would display a Confirm File Save dialog box asking if you want to replace the existing copy of the file.

If you are connected to the Internet through a dial-up provider service, you can disconnect from the service at this time.

Removing Links

The Eat Cetera Catering template contains many links to a page named nowhere.html on the Netscape server. The purpose of these links is only to suggest to you where you might add your own links. You can remove links individually or as a group. Perform the steps on the next page to remove the links on the Eat Cetera Catering page.

Steps To Remove Links

1 **Scroll down the page and point to the linked text, Golden Anniversary.**

The URL of the linked page displays at the bottom of the Composer window (Figure 2-29).

linked text (underlined, blue)

URL of linked text

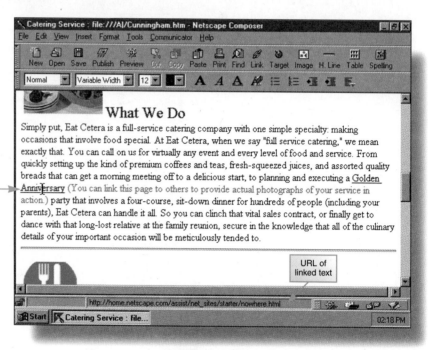

FIGURE 2-29

2 **Right-click the linked text and then point to Remove Link on the pop-up menu that displays.**

The linked text is selected (high-lighted) and a pop-up menu displays (Figure 2-30).

selected (highlighted) text

pop-up menu

Remove Link command

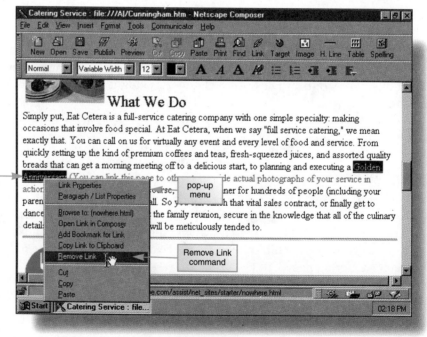

FIGURE 2-30

3 Click Remove Link and then click any other area on the page.

The link is removed and the text's color changes from the link text color to the normal text color (Figure 2-31).

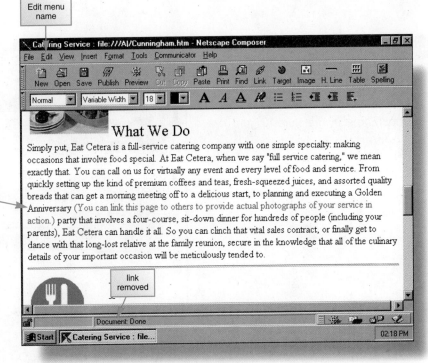

FIGURE 2-31

4 Click Edit on the menu bar and then point to Select All.

The Edit menu displays (Figure 2-32).

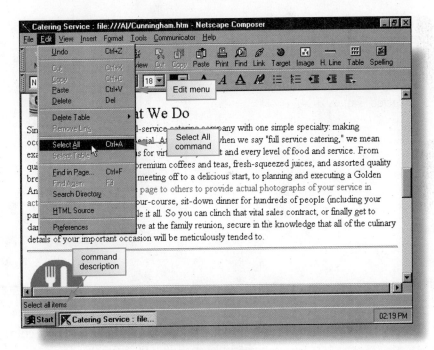

FIGURE 2-32

5 Click Select All. Click Edit on the menu bar and then point to Remove Link.

The entire page is selected for applying editing features (Figure 2-33).

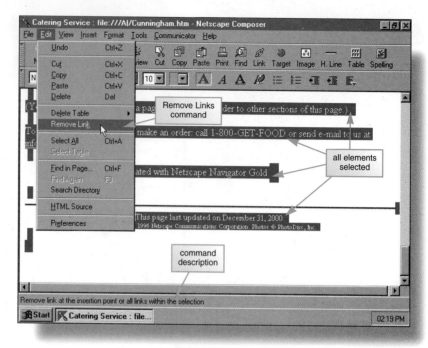

FIGURE 2-33

6 Click Remove Link and then click any area on the page.

All links within the page are removed and the page is deselected (Figure 2-34).

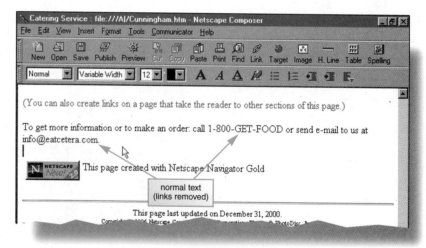

FIGURE 2-34

When you remove links, the text color changes to the normal text color specified in the Preferences dialog box.

Entering and Changing Text

You enter and modify text in Composer in ways that are very similar to working with word processing software such as Microsoft Word. The template work sheet you created is shown again in Figure 2-35. In the next series of steps, you will edit the text in the template as identified on your work sheet.

become a reality was provided by a chance encounter with another former college classmate, Maria Shapiro - fresh out of MBA school, dreaming of a business that she could back wholeheartedly, and still enchanted by the memories of meals at Mimi and Dana's apartment. (Use links to provide relevant biographical information.)

Delete

- To order
- Seminars and off-sites
- Weddings
- Parties

(You can also create links on a page that take the reader to other sections of this page.)

Target: contact

Contact Us

555-5555

To get more information or to make an order: call 1-800-GET FOOD or send e-mail to us at } *address format*

info@eatcetera.com.

cc@busserve.com ← *(bold)*

 This page created with Netscape Navigator Gold

September 25, 1998

This page last updated on December 31, 2000.

How to use this template
To use a Netscape Web page template in Navigator Gold, select the Edit Document command from the File menu to download the template to your hard drive so that you can edit it. Then customize the template with your own content. Please note that our suggestions serve only as place holders for your own information - the links are not real. Once your page is complete, be sure to delete all extraneous text (including this paragraph), as well as sample logos, links, images, and email addresses. Then you can post your page to the Internet using Navigator Gold's Publish feature.

Delete

Cunningham ←

Eat Cetera Catering

- Our Service
- What We Do
- Our Palette
- Contact Us

(Linked list to Targets on page)

(Remove All other Links)

Target! service

 Planning a seminar, off-site, party, wedding, or anniversary? Whatever the event, when it's important that you feel confident about the food - and the food service - Eat Cetera is the answer.

↑

(Replace All with Cunningham Catering)

What We Do

Target! do

 Simply put, Eat Cetera is a full-service catering company with one simple specialty: making occasions that involve food special. At Eat Cetera, when we say "full service catering," we mean exactly that. You can call on us for virtually any event and every level of food and service. From quickly setting up the kind of premium coffees and teas, fresh-squeezed juices, and assorted quality breads that can get a morning meeting off to a delicious start, to planning and executing a Golden Anniversary (You can link this page to others to provide actual photographs of your service in action.) party that involves a four-course, sit-down dinner for hundreds of people (including your parents), Eat Cetera can handle it all. So you can clinch that vital sales contract, or finally get to dance with that long-lost relative at the family reunion, secure in the knowledge that all of the culinary details of your important occasion will be meticulously tended to.

The Eat Cetera Palette

Target! palette

Short of letting you actually taste our food, it's hard to convey the appeal of our menu offerings - let alone the style of their presentation. For more casual affairs, Eat Cetera features a variety of continental buffet breakfast, and buffet and box lunch options. And our more elaborate meals let you mix and match from the broad palette of appetizers, salads, soups, entrees, and desserts that you'll find on our full dinner menu. (Link to pages that detail your offerings.) In addition, if you require setup, service, and cleanup, we can supply the works - plates, utensils, and highly trained servers.

Who We Are

Delete

A success since 1993, Eat Cetera is the brainchild of two former college dormmates - Mimi Treat and Dana Flynn -who fled the dorms largely because they wanted better food. The urge to eat well soon turned into an obsession, which led Dana to cooking school in Paris and Mimi to New York's Culinary Arts School. In 1992, continued correspondence about life goals reunited the two, who determined to create a catering company that went well beyond the ordinary. The final touch that allowed their goal to

FIGURE 2-35

Deleting Text and Horizontal Lines

As you move the mouse pointer over text in the Composer window, it displays as an **I-beam**. When you click the mouse, a blinking insertion point indicates the point where the next typed text will display in the window. When you press the DELETE key, the character following the insertion point is deleted. When you want to delete more than one or two characters, it is more efficient to select the text to be deleted and then press the DELETE key.

To select text, you can drag through the text. You can select a horizontal line by clicking it. Several ways to select different portions of text with the mouse also are available. Clicking before a line selects the entire line. Double-clicking a word selects the word. Double-clicking before a line selects the entire paragraph. Perform the following steps to select and delete horizontal lines and sections of text.

Steps To Select and Delete Text and Horizontal Lines

1 Scroll to the top of the page and then point to the left of the first horizontal line as shown in Figure 2-36.

The mouse pointer displays in the shape of a block arrow (Figure 2-36)

mouse pointer in left margin

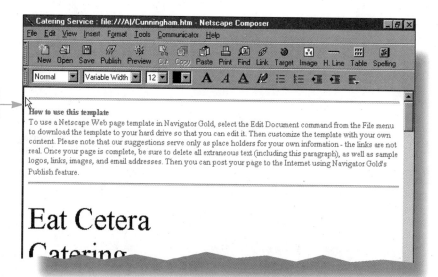

FIGURE 2-36

2 Drag down through the second horizontal line.

The entire paragraph including the horizontal lines above and below it are selected (Figure 2-37).

selection highlighted

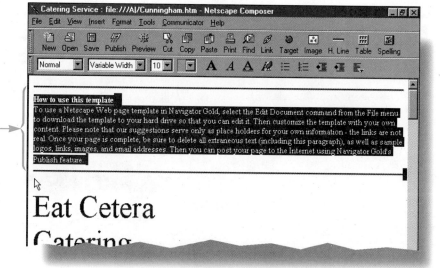

FIGURE 2-37

3 Press the DELETE key.

The selected paragraph and horizontal lines are deleted (Figure 2-38).

selection deleted from page

FIGURE 2-38

4 Scroll down the page and then drag through the text shown in Figure 2-39.

The text is selected (Figure 2-39).

text selected for deletion

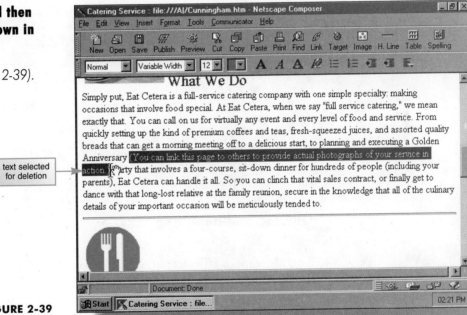

FIGURE 2-39

5 Press the DELETE key.

The text is deleted (Figure 2-40).

selected text deleted

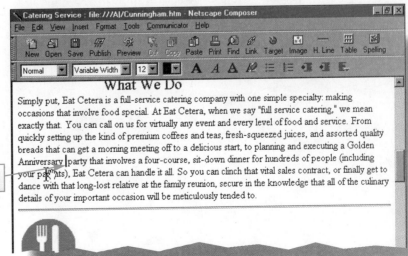

FIGURE 2-40

6 Scroll down the page and then delete the remaining sections identified for deletion on the work sheet (Figure 2-35 on page NC 2.25).

The end of the page should display as shown in Figure 2-41.

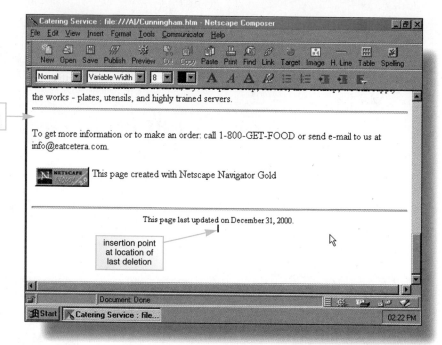

FIGURE 2-41

If you accidentally delete text, you can restore it by clicking Undo on the Edit menu. Unlike some word processors, however, you can only undo the last function you performed.

Finding and Replacing Text

You can replace a section of text by deleting the text and then typing new text. It is more efficient, however, simply to select the text to be replaced and then type the new text. Selected text can be copied to the Windows Clipboard and then pasted into another area of the document as well.

You can enter text into your document by **pasting** from almost any source. For example, you can select text on a page you are viewing in the browse window and copy it with the Copy command on the Edit menu. You then can paste it into the page you currently are editing by clicking Paste on the Edit menu. Perform the following steps to replace Eat Cetera Catering with Cunningham Catering and then modify the page's signature information.

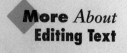

More *About* **Editing Text**

After you select a word or paragraph, you can drag and drop it anywhere in the Composer window. You can select a single word by double-clicking the word. You can select a paragraph by double-clicking to the left of the first word in the paragraph.

Steps **To Find and Replace Text**

---

1 **Scroll to the top of the page and then point to the left of the E in Eat.**

The I-beam mouse pointer displays (Figure 2-42)

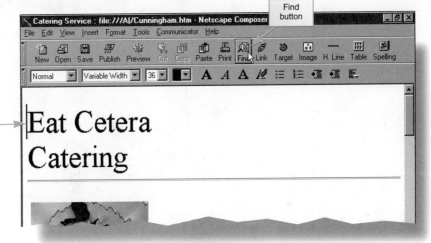

FIGURE 2-42

2 **Click and then point to the Find button on the Composition toolbar.**

The insertion point displays (Figure 2-43).

FIGURE 2-43

3 **Click the Find button, type** eat cetera **in the Find what text box, and point to the Find Next button.**

The Find dialog box displays (Figure 2-44).

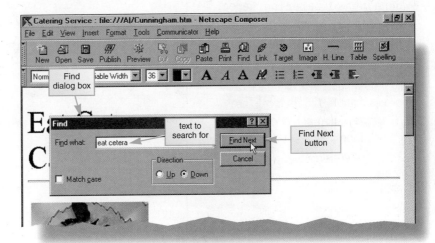

FIGURE 2-44

4 Click the Find Next button and then click the Close button in the Find dialog box.

The dialog box closes and the first occurrence of Eat Cetera is selected (Figure 2-45).

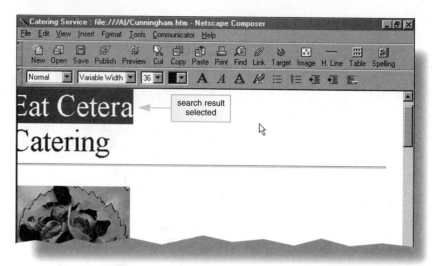

FIGURE 2-45

5 Press the DELETE. key. Press the DOWN ARROW key. Type Cunningham and then press the SPACEBAR.

The first occurrence of Eat Cetera is replaced with the new name (Figure 2-46).

FIGURE 2-46

6 Press the F3 key, and then type Cunningham Catering. Repeat this step five times until the Netscape dialog box displays.

Pressing the F3 key moves the highlight automatically to the next occurrence of the text to replace. The Netscape dialog box informs you that no more occurrences can be found (Figure 2-47).

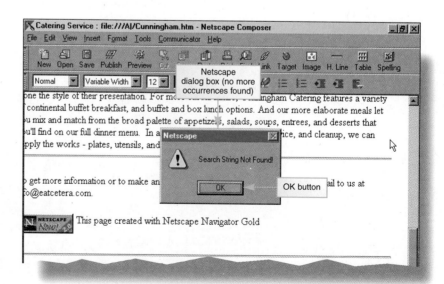

FIGURE 2-47

7 Click the OK button. Click to the right of the first horizontal rule above the paragraph that begins, To Get more information... to produce the insertion point and then press the ENTER key. Type Contact Us on the new line.

A new line is inserted and the text displays as normal text (Figure 2-48).

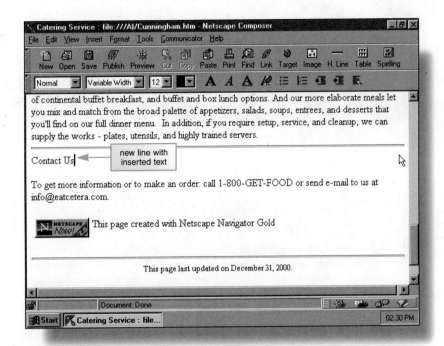

FIGURE 2-48

8 Type 1-800-555-5555 as the new number. Type cc@busserve.com as the new e-mail address. Type today's date.

The page displays as shown in Figure 2-49.

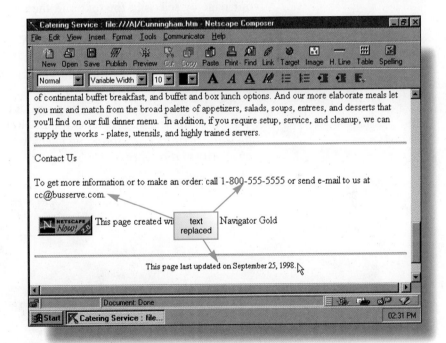

FIGURE 2-49

The reason you did not copy the words, Cunningham Catering, to the Clipboard and then paste them into the different locations is because the text would retain its original formatting features when pasted into the different locations. When you replace text as you did in the preceding steps, the new text has the same formatting as the text it replaces.

Setting Character Properties

You can apply formatting features called **character properties** to one or more characters, words, or paragraphs. These properties include font size and color. You can change the font itself (such as Arial or Times New Roman) with Composer. Composer also provides several **character styles** you can use to make your pages more interesting. These character styles include bold, italic, fixed width, superscript, subscript, blink, and underline.

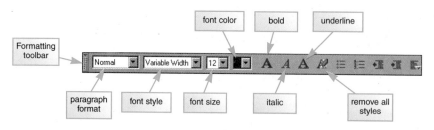

FIGURE 2-50

The Format menu contains character property settings. You are likely to find it easier, however, to use either the Formatting toolbar (Figure 2-50) or the Character sheet in the Character Properties dialog box (Figure 2-51). You can see from the two figures that not all of the character style settings in the dialog box have corresponding buttons on the toolbar.

You can change the character properties of any portion of existing text on your page by selecting the text and then applying the properties using the toolbar or Properties dialog box. When entering new text, you can choose between two methods to apply character properties. You can set character properties on the toolbar or in the dialog box first, in which case all new characters you type will have those properties, or you can type the text without properties, select it, and then apply properties.

When you enter formatted text in the first way described, you can return to typing unformatted text by clicking the Remove All Styles button on the Formatting toolbar or its corresponding check box in the Character Properties dialog box. Perform the following steps to set character properties on the Cunningham Catering page.

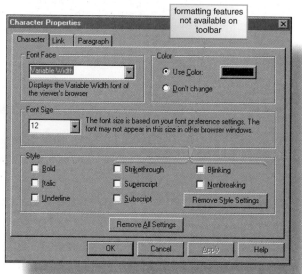

FIGURE 2-51

Steps **To Set Character Properties**

---

1 **Select the text, Contact Us, and then click the Font Color box arrow on the Formatting toolbar. Point to the color shown in Figure 2-52.**

The Color list box displays. The arrangement of custom colors may be different on your computer (Figure 2-52).

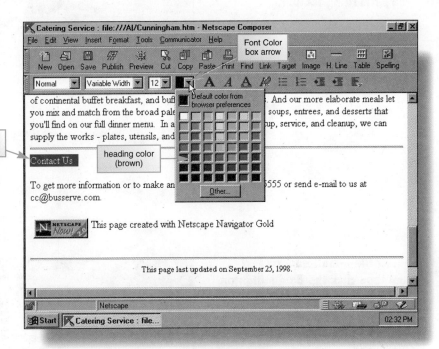

FIGURE 2-52

2 **Click the color brown (row 5, column 2) that matches the color of the headings on the template. Click the Font Size box arrow and then point to 18.**

The new color is applied but is not visible because the text is still selected (Figure 2-53).

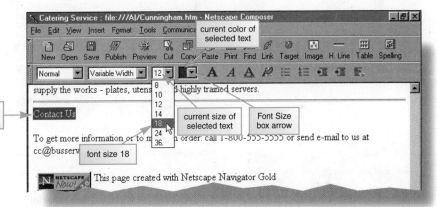

FIGURE 2-53

3 **Click 18.**

The size of the text is increased and displays in the Font Size box (Figure 2-54).

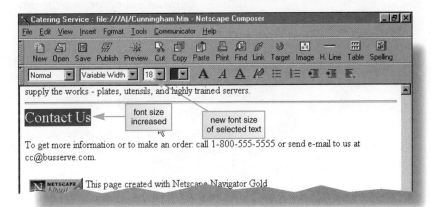

FIGURE 2-54

4 **Select the telephone number text and then click the Bold button on the Formatting toolbar.**

The telephone number is bolded (Figure 2-55).

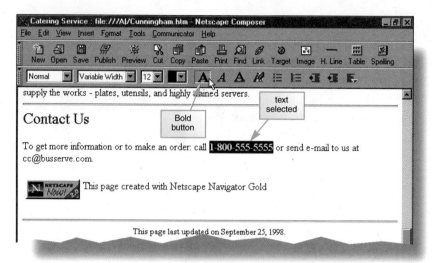

FIGURE 2-55

5 **Select the e-mail address text and then click the Bold button on the Formatting toolbar. Click anywhere in the Composer window to deselect the text.**

The page displays as shown in Figure 2-56.

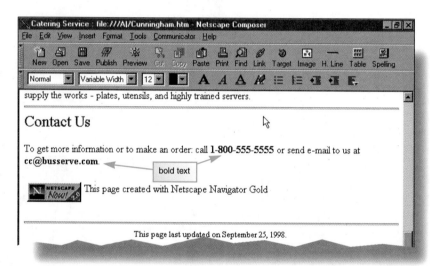

FIGURE 2-56

OtherWays

1. Select text to be formatted; double-click selected text, right-click Character Properties on pop-up menu, enter appropriate settings in Character Properties dialog box

If you prefer to set character properties with the Character Properties dialog box, you can open the Character Properties dialog box by clicking Character Properties on the Format menu, or right-clicking text in the edit area and then clicking Character Properties on the pop-up menu.

Formatting Paragraphs and Creating Lists

In the preceding section, you set properties for individual characters or groups of characters, such as words. You can apply additional formatting features to entire paragraphs. **Paragraph properties** include alignment, indenting, creating lists, and paragraph styles. The available **paragraph styles** and a description of each is listed in Table 2-1.

Table 2-1

PARAGRAPH STYLE	DESCRIPTION
Normal	Applies special formatting
Heading (1-6)	Formats the entire paragraph as a heading of size 1-6
Address	Formats the Signature section of a Web page
Formatted	Formats the text leaving spaces, tabs, and returns
List Item	Formats the text in a special list with a symbol (number or bullet) preceding the item
Description Title	Pairs left-aligned short entries with longer blocks of indented text
Description Text	Formats a single word or line associated with a block of indented text

Setting Paragraph Properties

You can use the **Paragraph submenu** of the Format menu to set paragraph properties. You are likely to find it easier, however, to use either the Formatting toolbar (Figure 2-57) or the Paragraph sheet in the Character Properties dialog box (Figure 2-58). You can see from the two figures that increasing and decreasing paragraph indents can be applied only through the corresponding buttons on the toolbar.

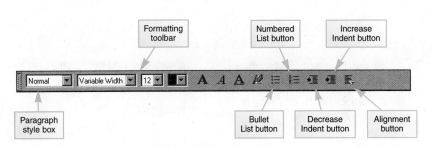

FIGURE 2-57

You can apply paragraph properties to just the paragraph where the insertion point is located or to multiple paragraphs that you have selected. Perform the steps on the next page to set paragraph properties on the Cunningham Catering page.

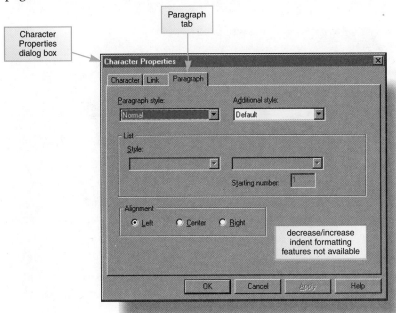

FIGURE 2-58

Steps **To Set Paragraph Properties**

1 **Double-click to the left of the T in the paragraph that begins, To get more information . . . .**

The paragraph is selected (Figure 2-59).

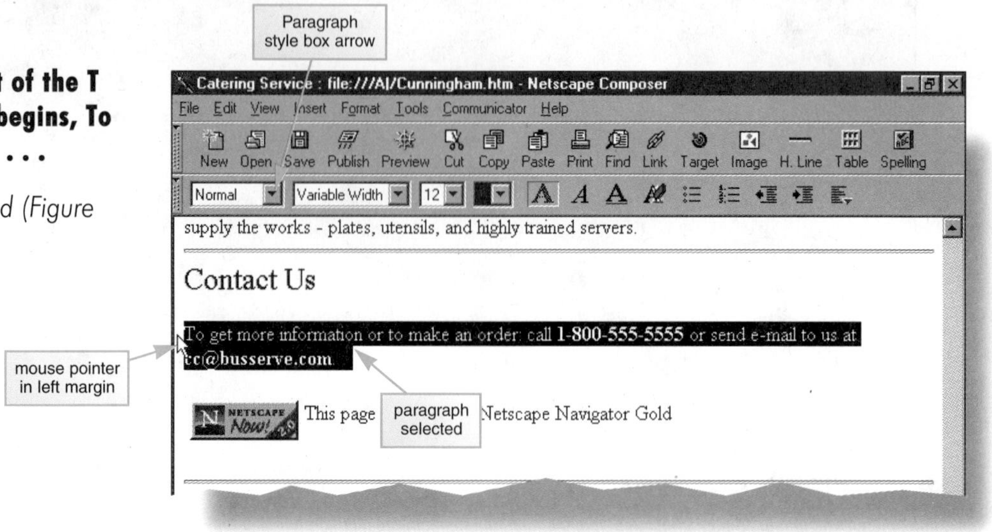

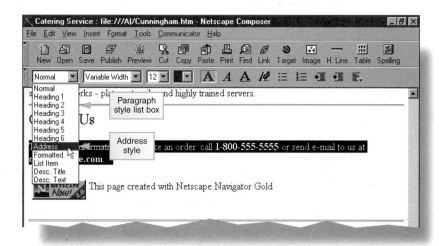

FIGURE 2-59

2 **Click the Paragraph style box arrow on the Formatting toolbar and then point to Address in the list of styles.**

The Paragraph style list box displays (Figure 2-60).

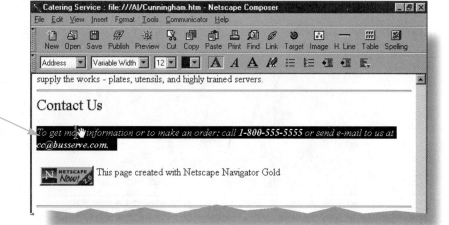

FIGURE 2-60

3 **Click Address.**

The paragraph is formatted to the Address style (Figure 2-61).

FIGURE 2-61

4 Scroll to the top of the page, click to the left of Cunningham Catering and then point to the Center button in the Alignment list.

The text is selected as one paragraph (Figure 2-62).

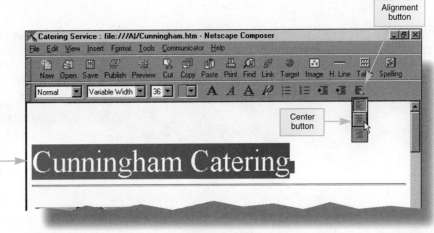

FIGURE 2-62

5 Click the Center button and then click the area below the horizontal rule to deselect the paragraph.

The text and horizontal rule are centered on the page (Figure 2-63).

FIGURE 2-63

In the preceding steps, you selected existing paragraphs and then applied formatting features. When you are typing a new paragraph, you can either set the paragraph properties and then type the new paragraph or first type the paragraph, and then select it and apply properties.

Creating Lists

The Formatting toolbar contains buttons for formatting bullet and numbered lists. In addition to these types of lists, several additional list styles are available to you using the Paragraph sheet of the Character Properties dialog box (Figure 2-64). The list styles available and a description of each are shown in Table 2-2 on the next page.

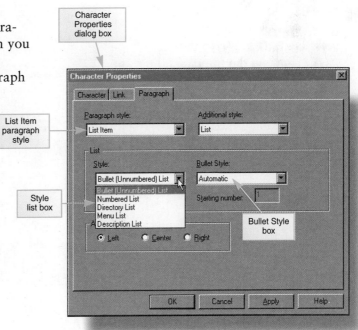

FIGURE 2-64

Table 2-2

LIST STYLE	DESCRIPTION
Bullet (Unnumbered List)	Items are preceded by a bullet or other symbol
Numbered List	Items are preceded by numbers or letters
Directory List	Short items that appear horizontally in columns
Menu List	Short items without numbers or bullets
Description List	Items are indented

It is common for a Web page to have a bullet list of the page's major headings located right after the title or introduction of the page. Items in the list are linked to the corresponding major sections of the document. The reader can use the list as a hypertext table of contents to move directly to a specific section of the page. Perform the following steps to add a bullet list of headings to the Cunningham Catering page.

Steps **To Add a Bullet List**

1 **Click to the right of the horizontal rule, press the ENTER key to begin a new paragraph, and click the Align Left button on the Formatting toolbar.**

The insertion point is left-aligned at the position of the new paragraph (Figure 2-65).

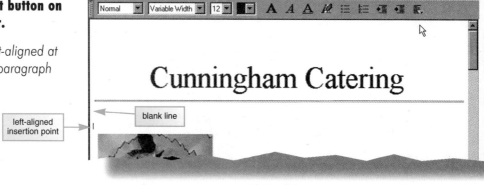

left-aligned insertion point

blank line

FIGURE 2-65

2 **Type** Our Service, **press the ENTER key, type** What We Do, **press the ENTER key, type** Our Palette, **press the ENTER key, type** Contact Us, **and press the ENTER key.**

The new text displays as shown in Figure 2-66.

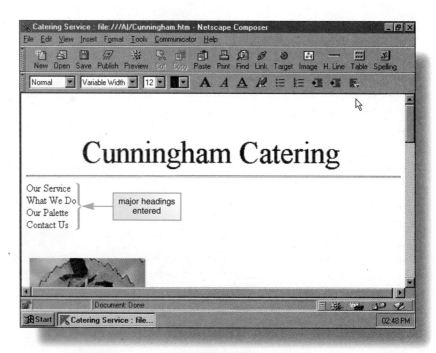

major headings entered

FIGURE 2-66

3 Select the four lines of text and then point to the Bullet List button on the Formatting toolbar.

The four lines are selected (Figure 2-67).

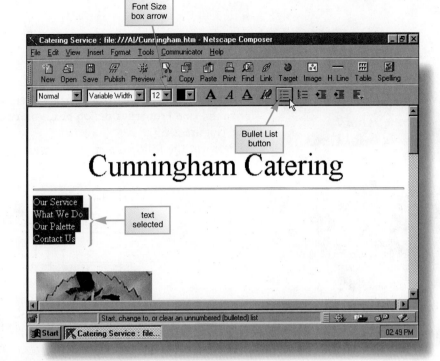

FIGURE 2-67

4 Click the Bullet List button. Click the Font Size box arrow, click 18, and then press the DOWN ARROW key.

The bullet list displays as shown in Figure 2-68.

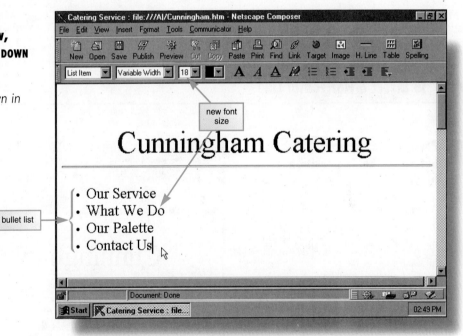

FIGURE 2-68

In the preceding steps, the **solid circle bullet style** was selected automatically. In addition, you can select open circle or solid square bullet styles on the Paragraph sheet of the Character Properties dialog box. Because the choice of bullet styles is limited, many Web pages actually use inline images as bullets for a list. You will learn how to use inline images as bullets in Project 3.

Inserting Horizontal Lines

Horizontal lines are used to set apart different sections of a Web page. Using the **Horizontal Line Properties dialog box**, you can set several properties of horizontal lines. (Figure 2-69).

Perform the following steps to insert a horizontal line below the bulleted list of topics on the Cunningham Catering page.

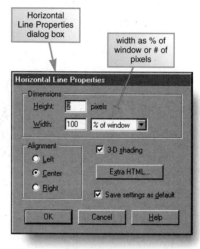

FIGURE 2-69

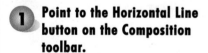 **To Insert a Horizontal Line**

1 **Point to the Horizontal Line button on the Composition toolbar.**

A blank line is entered and the insertion point moves to the beginning of the next line (Figure 2-70).

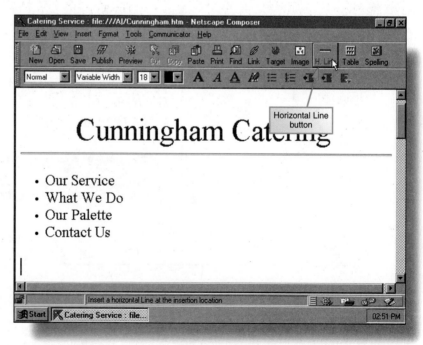

FIGURE 2-70

2 Click the Horizontal Line button.

Netscape inserts a horizontal (Figure 2-71).

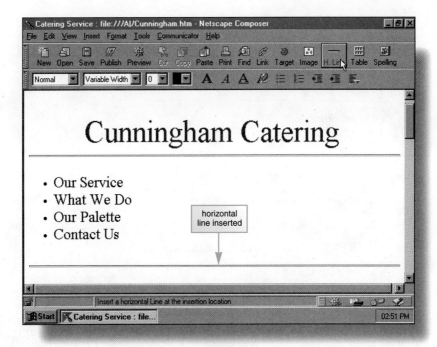

FIGURE 2-71

As you can see in the Horizontal Line Properties dialog box in Figure 2-69, not many variations are available for horizontal lines. For this reason, many Web pages use inline images for horizontal lines.

Adding Targets and Links to Targets

A Web page can contain **links** to other places on the page, such as the beginning of a new section, for example. These places are marked in HTML with an **anchor**. Netscape refers to these places as **targets**. Targets are identified by unique names that you assign. Targets are especially useful in aiding navigation through a long page.

Although the Cunningham Catering page is not very long, Mary wants to have the bullet list of headings linked to sections of the page. The locations and names of the targets are identified on the work sheet (Figure 2-72 on the next page).

Perform the steps on the next page to insert targets and then create links to those targets from the bullet list.

> **More** *About* **Targets**
>
> Targets provide a quick way for readers to jump to a specific place in your Web page. If your page is very long with many targets, however, you should consider breaking it into several smaller pages.

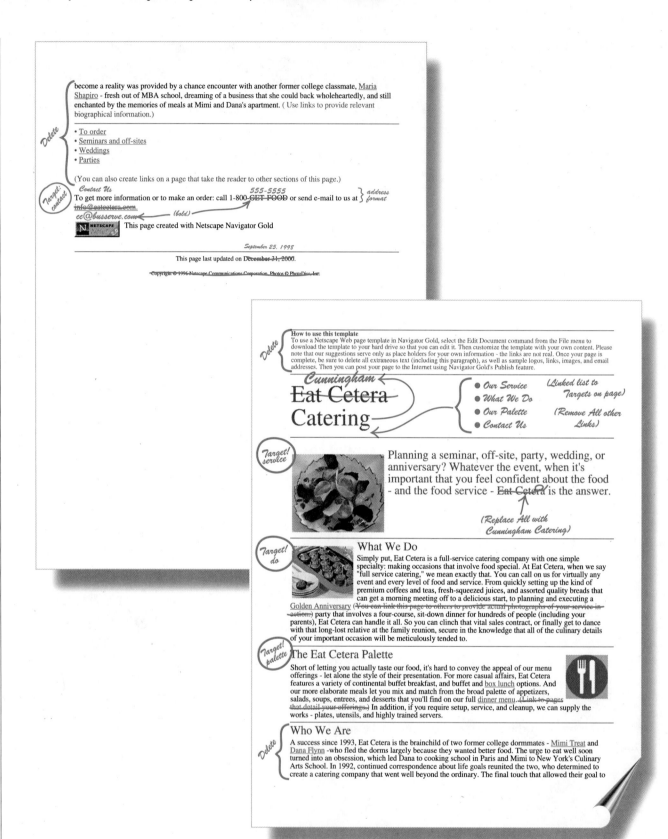

FIGURE 2-72

Steps **To Insert a Linked Target**

1 **Scroll down and click the lower-left corner of the first image on the page. Point to the Target button on the Composition toolbar.**

The insertion point is to the left of the image (Figure 2-73)

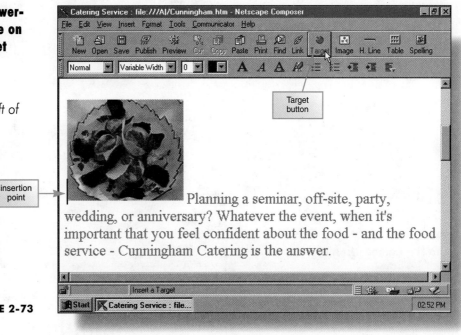

FIGURE 2-73

2 **Click the Target button and then type** service **in the Enter a name for this target text box.**

The Target Properties dialog box displays (Figure 2-74). A target has only one property, its name.

FIGURE 2-74

3 **Click the OK button.**

A target image is inserted in the edit window (Figure 2-75). It will not display in the browser.

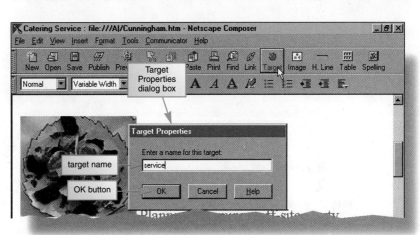

FIGURE 2-75

4 Repeat Steps 2 and 3 for each of the three remaining targets identified on the worksheet (Figure 2-72).

Target images are inserted in each location (Figure 2-76)

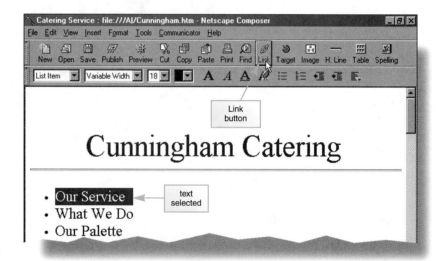

FIGURE 2-76

5 Scroll to the top of the page. Select the first bullet list item and then point to the Link button on the Composition toolbar.

The text, Our Service, is selected (Figure 2-77).

FIGURE 2-77

6 Click the Link button and then point to service in the Select a named target in current page list box.

The Character Properties dialog box displays with the Link sheet selected (Figure 2-78).

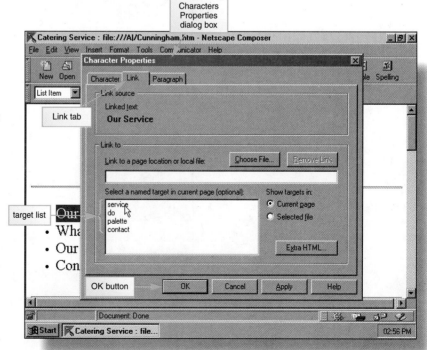

FIGURE 2-78

7 Click service and then click the OK button.

The Character Properties dialog box closes and the selected text displays underlined in the link text color (Figure 2-79).

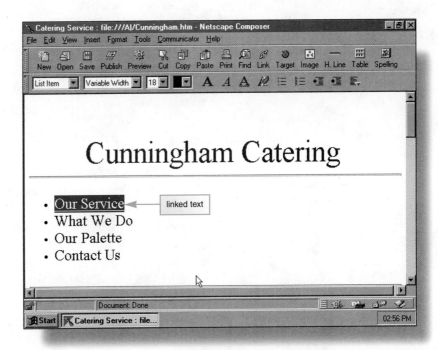

FIGURE 2-79

8 Repeat Steps 5,6, and 7 for the remaining items in the list and their corresponding targets.

All items in the list display as linked text (Figure 2-80).

FIGURE 2-80

The Link button and Link sheet in the Character Properties dialog box are used for making links not only to targets on the same page, but to other pages as well. Linking to other pages will be covered in Project 3.

Other Ways

1. Select text to be the linked, right-click selected text, click Create Link Using Selected on pop-up menu

Saving and Testing the Page

The Cunningham Catering Web page is complete. Perform the following steps to save the page and test it in the browser.

TO SAVE AND TEST THE PAGE

1. Click the Save button on the Composition toolbar.
2. Click the Preview button on the Composition toolbar.
3. Scroll through and view the page in the browser.
4. Test the links.
5. Click the Close button in the Navigator window.
6. Click the Close button in the Composer window.

Project Summary

Project 2 introduced you to the basic features of Composer. You first set some of the Composer preferences. After saving a remote template document locally, you edited the document. You added and deleted text in the document. You applied character and paragraph formatting features. You then created a linked list to targets within the page. After editing the template, you saved it and tested it.

What You Should Know

Having completed this project, you now should be able to perform the following tasks:

- Add a Bullet List *(NC 2.38)*
- Arrange the Toolbars *(NC 2.16)*
- Find and Replace Text *(NC 2.29)*
- Insert a Horizontal Line *(NC 2.40)*
- Insert a Linked Target *(NC 2.43)*
- Open an Composer Window *(NC 2.14)*
- Open a Remote Template in Composer *(NC 2.18)*
- Remove Links *(NC 2.22)*
- Save and Test the Page *(NC 2.46)*
- Select and Delete Text and Horizontal Lines *(NC 2.26)*
- Set Character Properties *(NC 2.33)*
- Set Composer Preferences *(NC 2.11)*
- Set Paragraph Properties *(NC 2.36)*

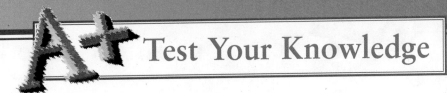

Test Your Knowledge

1 True/False

Instructions: Circle T if the statement is true or F if the statement is false.

T F 1. Web page templates always are remote documents.

T F 2. Everything on the Internet is copyrighted.

T F 3. The default template file is set in the document preferences.

T F 4. The Netscape Composer has three toolbars.

T F 5. Composer toolbars can float in the edit area.

T F 6. Pressing the ENTER key in Composer inserts a paragraph tag in the HTML source.

T F 7. Composer provides a search and replace tool.

T F 8. Pressing the SHIFT+ENTER keys in Composer advances to a new line without inserting a paragraph tag in the HTML source.

T F 9. You can choose different font styles (typefaces) in Composer.

T F 10. Opening a Composer window closes all browse windows.

2 Multiple Choice

Instructions: Circle the correct response.

1. In Composer, font sizes range from _____.
   - a. 0 to 4
   - b. 8 to 36
   - c. 12 to 48
   - d. -2 to +4

2. Of the following, which is *not* a paragraph style?
   - a. Address
   - b. Formatted
   - c. Description List
   - d. Description Text

3. Another term for a target is a _____.
   - a. link
   - b. named anchor
   - c. hypertext reference
   - d. bullet

4. To save a remote template while viewing it in the browser, click File on the menu bar and then click _____.
   - a. Edit
   - b. View in Composer
   - c. Document Source
   - d. Save

5. Of the following, which is *not* bullet style?
   - a. open circle
   - b. solid square
   - c. solid circle
   - d. open square

6. Of the following, which is *not* a horizontal line property?
   - a. width
   - b. alignment
   - c. shading
   - d. color

7. Copyrighted material can be used if you can meet the _____ test.
   - a. ceteris paribus
   - b. statute of limitations
   - c. fair use
   - d. none of the above

(continued)

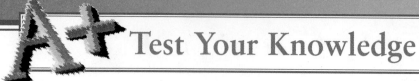

Test Your Knowledge

Multiple Choice *(continued)*

8. Of the following, which is *not* a Preferences dialog box category?
   a. Composer
   b. General
   c. Publish
   d. Appearance

9. Of the following character properties, which one *cannot* be set from the toolbar?
   a. fixed width
   b. strikethrough
   c. underline
   d. italic

10. Linked text _____.
    a. is always blue
    b. always changes color after the link is activated
    c. is always underlined
    d. none of the above

3 Understanding the Formatting Toolbar

Instructions: In Figure 2-81, arrows point to several buttons on the Formatting toolbar. In the spaces provided, briefly explain the purpose of each button.

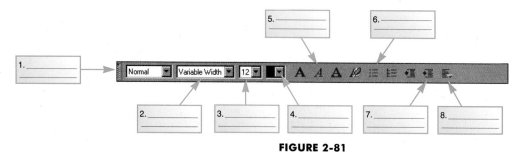

FIGURE 2-81

4 Understanding the Composition Toolbar

Instructions: In Figure 2-82, arrows point to several buttons on the Composition toolbar. In the spaces provided, briefly explain the purpose of each button.

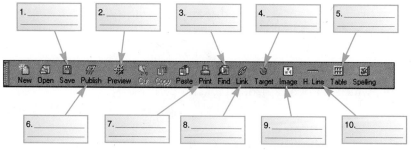

FIGURE 2-82

Use Help

1 Using Netscape Help

Instructions: Start Netscape Communicator, and perform the following tasks with a computer.

1. Open a Composer window.
2. Click the Character Properties command on the Format toolbar.
3. Click the Paragraph tab in the Properties dialog box.
4. Click the Help button in the Properties dialog box.
5. Read the Help file.
6. What is the difference between the Apply and Close buttons in Composer dialog box windows?
7. Print your answer and turn it in to your instructor.

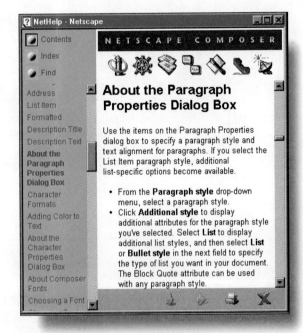

FIGURE 2-83

2 Netscape's Page Starter Site

Instructions: Start Netscape Composer and perform the following tasks with a computer.

1. Click Product Information and Support on the Help menu.
2. Scroll down the page and click Web Page Starter.
3. Scroll down the page and click Web Page templates.
4. Scroll down and click any one of the links under the Copyrights category.
5. Explore the page.
6. Write a brief summary of what you found and turn it in to your instructor.

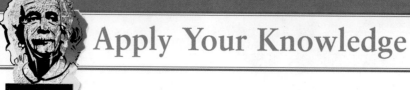

1 Editing the Apply Your Knowledge Web Page

Instructions: Figure 2-84 shows the Apply Your Knowledge Web Page as it should appear in the Netscape browser. Apply-2 is a file containing text, but without any formatting. Perform the following activities.

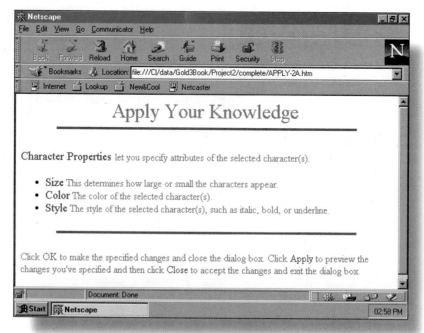

FIGURE 2-84

1. Start Netscape.
2. Open the file Apply-2 in a Composer window.
3. Apply the appropriate character and paragraph properties for the page to display as shown in Figure 2-84.
4. Save the file, giving it the name ApplyKnowledge2.
5. Print the revised document.
6. Write your name on the printout and hand it in to your instructor.

In the Lab

1 Removing Links and Extraneous Text from a Template

Problem: You have decided to use Netscape's Job Listings template. The template has links to targets within the page that you want to keep. You want to remove any links to other pages and delete any extraneous text such as the suggestions on how to use the template that are inserted throughout the page.

Instructions: Perform the following tasks.

1. Start Netscape. Click File on the menu bar and then click New. Click Page From Template on the New submenu. Click Netscape Templates.
2. Click the link to the Job Listings template.
3. Click File on the menu bar and then click Edit.
4. Name the template LAB2-1.
5. Delete the How to use this template section, including the horizontal lines above and below it.
6. Delete all of the Netscape suggestions on the page.
7. Remove any links to other pages (do not remove links to targets within the page).
8. Replace the date at the bottom of the page with today's date.
9. Save the page and print the page.
10. Write your name on the printout and turn it in to your instructor.

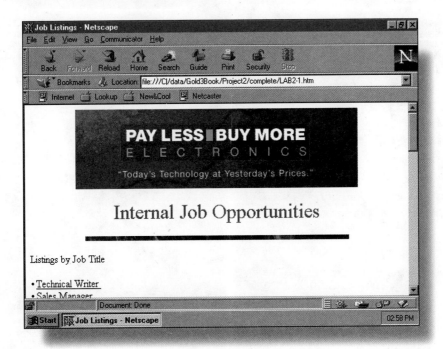

FIGURE 2-85

In the Lab

2 Adding Targets and Links to Targets

Problem: You have decided to use Netscape's Windsurfing Club template. You will be making more modifications later, but first you want to add a bullet list of links to the four sections of the page.

Instructions: Perform the following tasks.

1. Start Netscape. Click File on the menu bar and then click New. Click From Template on the New submenu. Click Netscape Templates.
2. Click the link to the Windsurfing Club template.
3. Click File on the menu bar and then click Edit.
4. Name the template LAB2-2.
5. Insert targets before each of the four section headings, giving them appropriate names.
6. Insert a bullet list of links to the targets at the beginning of the page (Figure 2-86).
7. Replace the date at the bottom of the page with today's date.
8. Save the page and print the page.
9. Write your name on the printout and turn it in to your instructor.

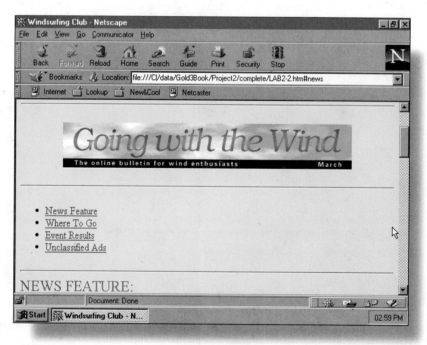

FIGURE 2-86

In the Lab

3 Changing Character and Paragraph Properties

Problem: You have decided to use Netscape's Department Overview template. You need to make some preliminary modifications to the page.

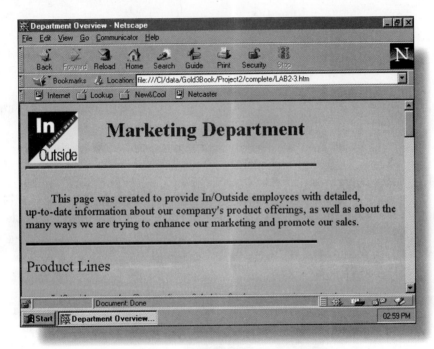

FIGURE 2-87

Instructions: Perform the following tasks.

1. Open Netscape's Department Overview template in Composer (its file name should be LAB2-3).
2. Delete extraneous text and remove all links.
3. Decrease the title's font size by one unit.
4. Format the first paragraph of text on the page as Description Text and format the last two paragraphs on the page with the Address style.
5. Select a blue on orange color scheme for the page (*Hint*: search Help on document properties).
6. Write your name on the printout of the page and turn it in to your instructor.

Cases and Places

The difficulty of these case studies varies: ❱ are the least difficult; ❱❱ are more difficult; and ❱❱❱ are the most difficult.

1 ❱ You would like to have your resume available on the Web. Use the same structure and format provided in the Resume template available from the Netscape Web Page Template page. Replace Clea's information with your own personal information (you can delete Clea's picture).

2 ❱ The Floribunda company would like to have the appearance of its Web page changed (use the Netscape Flower and Garden Supplies template). The management has contracted you to make changes. Develop at least two different versions of the current page, changing only the character and paragraph properties of various sections of the page.

3 ❱❱ The Human Resources department currently has a Web page (use the Netscape Human resources template), but the directors would like you to modify it for the department. They would like to keep the same information and format, but they want a bullet list of links to the different sections of the page located at the top of the page.

4 ❱❱ Your entrepreneur friend wants to pursue his idea of *gag* Web pages. Find any prominent company's or person's Web page and customize it with information about a friend. What are the copyright issues if you do this as a class exercise without publishing the page versus if your friend starts to sell the *gag* pages and publish them on the Web?

5 ❱❱❱ A friend of yours has asked you to create a home page for her. Print the Netscape My Home Page template. You meet with your friend to discuss the printout and determine what she would like to have and what you are able to do at this point. Create a home page for your friend.

6 ❱❱❱ Although Netscape Communications Corporation makes a number of good Web page templates, it is not the only source of templates on the Internet. Search the Internet for another source of templates. Decide on one you like. Customize it to your liking (you can use your own fictitious information).

7 ❱❱❱ Find a local business or organization that does not have a Web page. Research information about that organization. Use an appropriate Web page template to build a page for that organization.

Netscape Composer

Creating and Publishing Custom Web Pages

Objectives:

You will have mastered the material in this project when you can:

▶ List major Web page design considerations
▶ Open a blank page in Composer
▶ Set page properties
▶ Set a Web page texture
▶ Insert tables
▶ Set table properties
▶ Insert images
▶ Set image properties
▶ Insert links to other Web pages
▶ Insert horizontal rule images
▶ Understand the function of JavaScript
▶ Insert HTML tags
▶ Publish a Web page

Web Page Design

Among the Great Composers

Are genius and madness truly twins? Literature abounds with examples of people who have had split personalities, one *self* pursuing all that is great and shining, the other leading to the depths of despair. In Robert Louis Stevenson's, *The Strange Case of Dr. Jekyll and Mr. Hyde*, a distinguished healer tries his own life potion on himself and transforms into a fiend. In *Faust*, Goethe suggests that men have two opposing souls.

Even stranger than fiction are two cases of real men, both noted composers of the nineteenth century, both with progressive deafness, and both having last names beginning with the letter S.

Robert Schumann, whose beautiful musical compositions still grace the world, had to spend the final years of his life in a mental institution, where many of the hundreds of his compositions were composed. In his diary,

DIE MOLDAU—*Smetana*

Schumann wrote that his hallucinations drove him to write, "glorious music with instruments sounding more wonderful than one ever hears on earth." Some of his best works, such as *Kreisleriana*, the *Spring* symphony, and the *Manfred Overture*, were written at the urging of inner voices coming from *angels who hovered over him*. As his deafness progressed, he would hear complete original scores in his mind, with the final chord ringing continuously until he forced himself either to write out the entire piece or go on to another composition.

One of Schumann's many famous musical contemporaries, Czechoslovakian composer Bedrich Smetana, also began to lose his hearing at the height of his fame. A continuous high-pitched E note from a violin — a condition now known as *tinnitus* — sounded inside his ear, driving him to madness. Yet, he continued to compose some of his more beautiful pieces. Today, Czechs consider this gifted composer of hundreds of works, including *The Bartered Bride*, *Ma Vlast* (*My Country*), and the lovely *Die Moldau*, to be their supreme national composer.

Finally, the Web page creation capabilities of Netscape Composer make it possible for you to join the company of great composers. Although, you are working with artistic document production, the finished product will leave a lasting impression on those who will view your page. While Web page composition is relatively young, definite design guidelines will ensure an attractive and tasteful work.

Before you begin, consider the purpose of your page and intended audience to help you shape information and content and select a consistent voice to address them. Structure your information. Put as much content toward the top level so the casual reader can grasp your concept. Group topics onto a single page. Decide on and test the links so browsers can navigate with ease. Consider the pizzazz of multimedia, but remember that the more complex your page, the more time you will need to create your finished work of art.

With your PC and Netscape Composer, you may find yourself among the great content composers of the World Wide Web.

Netscape Composer

Creating and Publishing Custom Web Pages

Case Perspective

Bob Davis plans to graduate next May. He has been using the World Wide Web as a source for job opportunities. Of the many employment and job search Web pages available, Bob has identified eight that he has found especially useful. Bob would like to share this knowledge with the rest of his classmates and anyone else who might be interested. He has decided that a Web page is the best way to do this.

Bob has drawn a sketch of his ideas for a Job Links Web page. Neither the Page Wizard nor any copyright-free templates he has found will fit his needs, so he has asked you to help build a custom page from scratch. Bob would like to have a nice-looking texture for the page. Bob wants several graphics, including an animated graphic and a graphic for a horizontal line. He also wants a two-column layout of the links to the job Web sites. In addition to a signature with an email link, he wants the current date and time displayed on the page. You have reviewed his ideas and a sketch he drew and have agreed to build the page for him.

Introduction

In this project, you will build and publish Bob's Job Links Web page (Figure 3-1). Before you begin the actual construction of any Web page, you should start by considering the purpose of the page and its intended audience. The purpose may be to share information about yourself (a home page) or information you have obtained about some area of interest or expertise. It may be to provide a discussion forum or to solicit ideas and opinions from others. You may want to sell a product or service or you simply might want to provide an entertaining place for Web surfers to stop for a while. You also should think about who you want to read your page. You may have a specific audience in mind, or you may just want to put it up for anyone who stops by.

Web Page Design Guidelines

You can learn a great deal about Web page design by studying pages you see on the Web. Avoid the temptation to view immediately the HTML source of a page you like. Instead, study the overall page, its color, aesthetics, and navigation. In short, try to list the design elements that make it an attractive and interesting page. Later, after you have decided on an overall design, you can go back and study the technical details of how a specific page was constructed.

You will have no trouble finding numerous books and Internet resources on Web page design. Although this book is not about graphic design of Web pages, a few important considerations are required. Keep your pages **concise**. If people reading your page cannot find what they want quickly, they will move to another page. Keep the content short and to the point.

Web pages should have a **consistent style**. Examples include using the same headline format on every page and using consistent colors for text and backgrounds. Use Web page elements in **moderation**. When you add every neat gimmick and animated image you can find, your page becomes distracting and confusing. Many background textures that are available make it almost impossible to read the text. Large images or a large number of images not only are confusing, they take a long time to load.

You also should consider the **display** of your page. Although

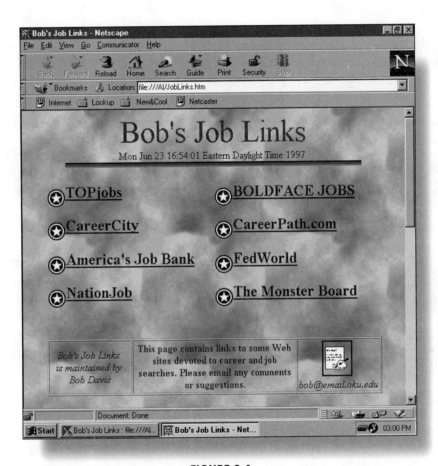

FIGURE 3-1

Internet Explorer and Netscape Navigator together account for more than 95 percent of the browser market, even these two **browsers** will display some HTML tags differently. Along with the browser your readers will use, you should consider **screen resolution**. An increasing number of pages on the Web are being designed for screen resolutions of 800x600 rather than 640x480.

Be prepared to **revise** your page even before it is finished. Do not be afraid to try many different arrangements of the same set of elements until you find just the right combination. Finally, you must realize that a good Web page is **never finished**. Not only is it important that you keep the content current, you must keep the design looking fresh and current also.

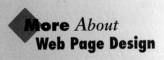

More *About*
Web Page Design

A large number of resources for Web page authors are available on the World Wide Web. For more sources of Web page design guidelines, visit the Composer Web site (www.scsite.com/nc/pr3.htm) and click the link to Design Guidelines.

Bob's Job Links
Date / Time

⭐ TOPjobs ⭐ BOLDFACE JOBS

⭐ CareerCity ⭐ CareerPath.com

⭐ America's Job Bank ⭐ FedWorld

⭐ NationJob ⭐ The Monster Board

| Bob's Job Links is maintained by Bob Davis | This page contains links to some Web sites devoted to career and job searches. Please email any comments or suggestions. | bob @email.oku.edu |

FIGURE 3-2

Project Three – Bob's Job Links

When you create a Web page for someone other than yourself, it is especially important to have a design specification to work from. Figure 3-2 shows a sketch of Bob's page on which you and he have agreed as the blueprint for your work. You will use the Web creation and editing capabilities of Netscape Composer to construct this page.

Project Steps

The following tasks will be completed in this project.

1. Open a Netscape browse window and download image files.
2. Open a Composer window with a blank page.
3. Set a background image and other page properties.
4. Insert tables and set table properties.
5. Insert images and set image properties.
6. Copy and paste an image.
7. Insert and format text.
8. Link text to other Web pages.
9. Insert an animated .gif file.
10. Create an email image link.
11. Save the page.
12. Drag and drop an image.
13. Insert HTML tags and JavaScript.
14. Save and test the page.
15. Publish a Web page.

More *About* **Clip Art Images**

One way to insure that the images you use in your pages are not copyrighted is to obtain them from the many free sources of clip art on the Web. For more information on sources of free clip art, visit the Composer Web site (www.scsite.com/nc/pr3.htm) and click the link to More Clip Art.

Downloading Image Files

Clip art images are graphic images that are available for you to use in your Web pages. Clip art images either may be free or may be offered for sale. Clip art can be found in file libraries or on Web pages. You can insert images into your Web pages from local files or you can drag and drop images from other Web pages. You will learn both of these methods in this project. To insert the images from local files, however, you first must download them from the Shelly Cashman Online Composer Web site. Perform the following steps to open a browse window and make local copies of several image files.

TO DOWNLOAD IMAGE FILES

1. Start Communicator and open the Composer Web site at www.scsite.com/nc/pr3.htm in a Netscape browse window.
2. Scroll down to Clipart.
3. Right-click the clouds image and then click Save Image As.
4. Save the image on a floppy disk in drive A.
5. Repeat Steps 3 and 4 for the bullet image and the mail image.

You should have the three image files shown in Figure 3-3 saved on a floppy disk in drive A.

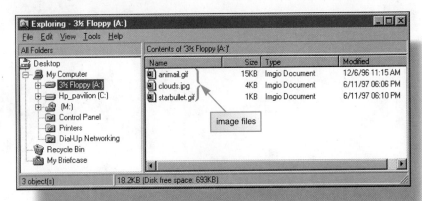

FIGURE 3-3

Whenever you make local copies of image files from other Web pages, you should be sure that no copyright restrictions exist on your use of them.

Opening a Composer Window with a Blank Page

In Project 1, you started a new page from Page Wizard. In Project 2, you started a new page from a template. In this project, you will start Composer with a new blank page. A Netscape Navigator browse window already is open on the desktop from downloading the image files. Perform the following steps to open a Composer window and start editing a new blank page.

 To Open a Composer Window with a Blank Page

1. **Click the Composer icon on the Communicator Component bar, close the Navigator browse window, and point to the New button on the Composer toolbar.**

   Netscape Composer starts and opens a window (Figure 3-4).

FIGURE 3-4

2 **Click the New button. When the Create New Page dialog box displays, point to the Blank Page button.**

The first three buttons in the Create New Page dialog box (Figure 3-5) produce the same results as the commands on the File/New submenu.

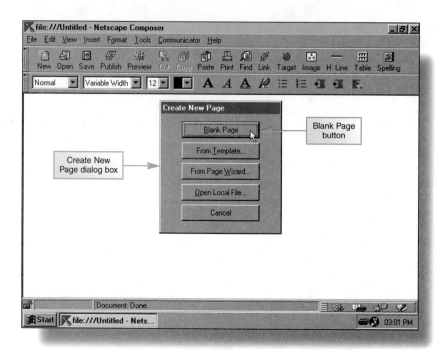

FIGURE 3-5

3 **Click the Blank Page button. Click Format on the menu bar and then point to Page Colors and Properties.**

Clicking the Blank Page button opens a second Composer window (Figure 3-6).

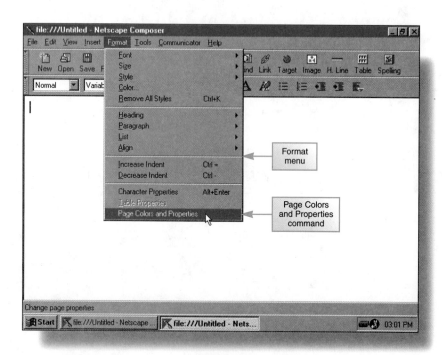

FIGURE 3-6

Other Ways

1. From Composer window, press CTRL+SHIFT+N

When Composer is started from the Component bar, it automatically starts with a new blank page. When you are working in a Composer window and you want to open another Composer window, you must specify that the new Composer window will start with a blank page, template, page wizard, or local file.

Setting a Background Image and Page Properties

A Web page **texture** refers to the background design of a Web page. Web page textures are created by tiling a small graphic image many times across the page. You use the **Page Properties dialog box** to set general information and properties for your documents such as author name, keywords, link colors, and background images and colors.

The **General panel** (Figure 3-7) is where you provide the page's title and other information helpful to Web users searching for specific topics. **Keywords** help users locate your document on the Web using search engines. **Classification names** also are used by search services to locate documents. You can obtain classification names from a Web catalog server.

You can specify to use the browser's colors for linked text and document background, or you can specify custom colors for the current document on the **Colors and Backgrounds panel** (Figure 3-8).

The Background button displays the color list box where you choose a solid color as the background for the current document. You also can specify an image file to be used for a background texture. Background images appear tiled and override background color selections. Perform the following steps to set page properties and set a texture for the JobLinks page.

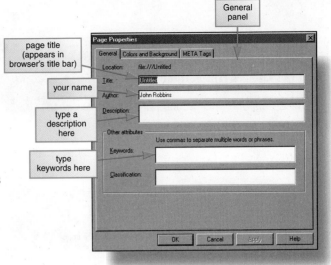

FIGURE 3-7

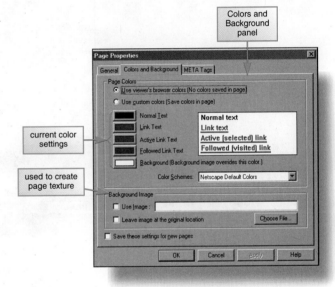

FIGURE 3-8

 Steps To Set Page Properties

1 **Click Page Colors and Properties and then point to the Colors and Background tab.**

The Page Properties dialog box opens with the General panel displayed (Figure 3-9). Your name should display in the Author text box. On the General panel, you can title the current page and set other properties.

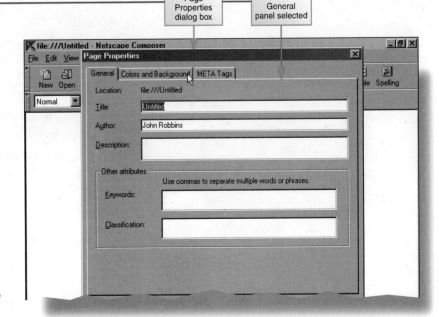

FIGURE 3-9

2 Click the Colors and Background tab, click Use Image, and point to the Choose File button.

The Colors and Background panel displays. You will keep the default values for link text colors (Figure 3-10).

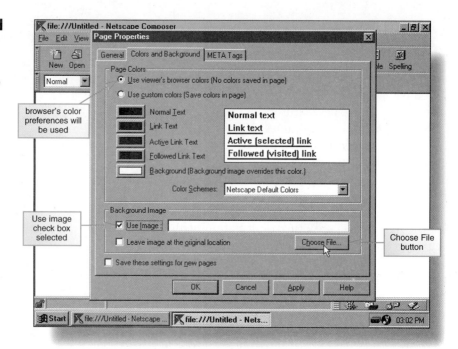

FIGURE 3-10

3 Click the Choose File button. When the Choose Image File dialog box opens, if necessary, click 3½ Floppy [A:] in the Look in list box, and then point to clouds.jpg (Figure 3-11).

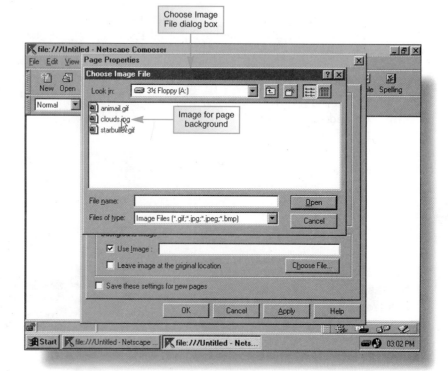

FIGURE 3-11

4 **Double-click clouds.jpg and then point to the OK button.**

The Choose Image File dialog box closes and the file name clouds.jpg displays in the Use Image text box (Figure 3-12).

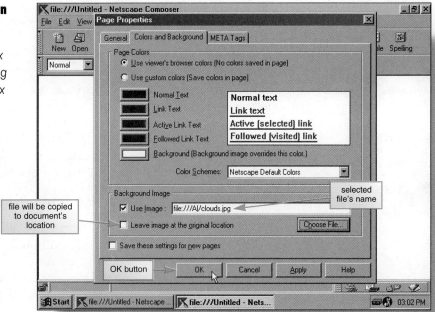

FIGURE 3-12

5 **Click the OK button.**

The clouds.jpg image is tiled across the Web page (Figure 3-13).

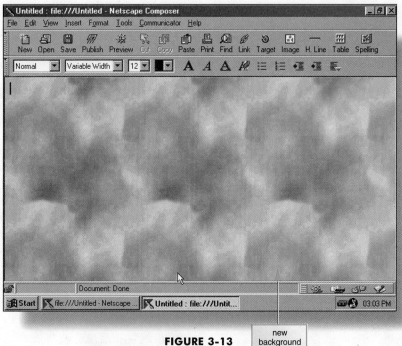

FIGURE 3-13

Most Web search tools locate pages by their titles. A meaningful title is important to ensure that people can find your page.

Other Ways

1. Right-click a blank area within Composer edit area, press G, click Colors and Background tab, press H

More *About*
Tables

Several advanced table formatting features that are available as HTML tag attributes are not supported directly by Composer. You can include these attributes, however, by clicking the Extra HTML button in the Table Properties dialog box and then typing them in the Extra HTML dialog box that displays.

Inserting Tables and Setting Table and Cell Properties

Tables are useful for presenting any information you want to display in a grid. Tables present information in rows and columns. Similar to a spreadsheet, the intersection is called a **cell**. Bob's page contains two tables. The lower table is easy to see, but the upper table is not visible in the browser (Figure 3-1 on page 3.5).

You can accomplish sophisticated page layouts (such as multi-column text) by using tables whose borders are not visible. You can even insert a table within the cell of another table (called **nesting**) for even greater layout control.

Inserting Tables and Setting Table Properties

In the **New Table Properties dialog box** (Figure 3-14), you can set the number of rows and columns, border line width, cell spacing and padding, table width and height, color, and captioning. A zero (0) value for border width makes the border invisible in a browser. Composer, however, displays tables with a zero (0) border width by using dotted lines. Cell padding sets the top, bottom, right, and left margins of each cell.

You can specify table width and height as either a percentage of the window width or as a number of pixels. If you specify the width as a percentage, the table's dimension changes whenever the browse window's dimension changes. You also can set a color for the table's background or you can specify an image for the table's background.

After a table has been inserted, you can modify its table properties by changing settings on the **Table panel** (Figure 3-15) in the Table Properties dialog box.

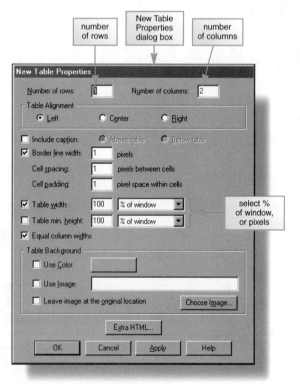

FIGURE 3-14

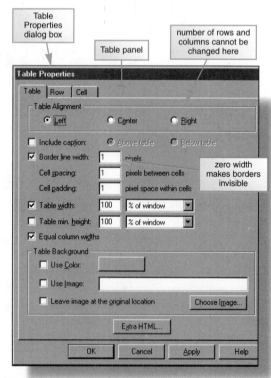

FIGURE 3-15

Perform the following steps to insert the first table in the JobLinks page and set its table properties.

Steps **To Insert a Table and Set Table Properties**

1 **Click the upper-left corner of the page and then point to the Table button on the Composition toolbar.**

The insertion point is the location where the table will be inserted (Figure 3-16).

FIGURE 3-16

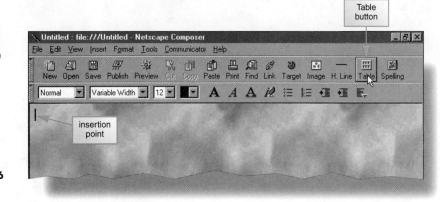

2 **Click the Table button.**

The New Table Properties dialog box displays (Figure 3-17).

FIGURE 3-17

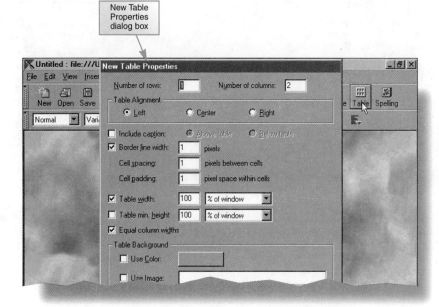

3 **Type 4 in the Number of rows text box. Click Center in the Table Alignment area. Type 0 in the Border line width text box. Type 90 in the Table width text box. Point to the OK button.**

The new property values display as shown in Figure 3-18.

FIGURE 3-18

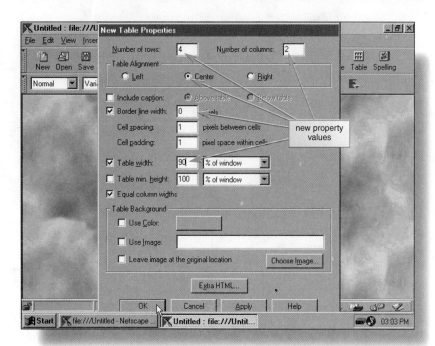

4 **Click the OK button.**

The new table is added to the Web page. Its borders display as dotted lines in the Composer window but will not appear when the page displays in the Navigator window. The text insertion point displays in the top left cell of the table (Figure 3-19).

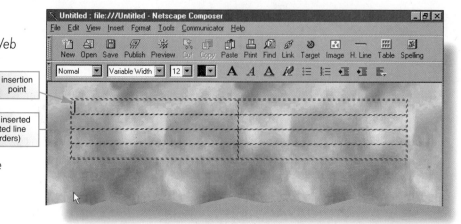

FIGURE 3-19

Other Ways

1. Press ALT+I, press T, press T

The Table panel is very similar to the New Table Properties dialog box, with one important exception. Once a table has been inserted, you cannot change the number of rows or columns on the Table panel. Instead, you must right-click the cell in the table where you want the addition or deletion to occur and then click Table, Row, Column, or Cell from either the Insert submenu or the Delete submenu.

Setting Row and Cell Properties

You can set properties that affect an entire row of cells or an individual cell by changing values on the **Row panel** (Figure 3-20) and **Cell panel** (Figure 3-21) in the Table Properties dialog box. **Row properties** include alignment and background color or image.

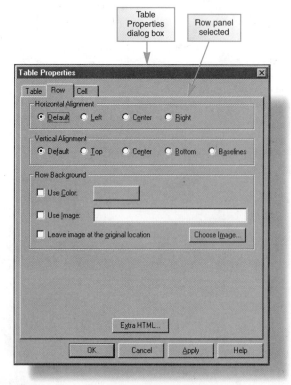

FIGURE 3-20

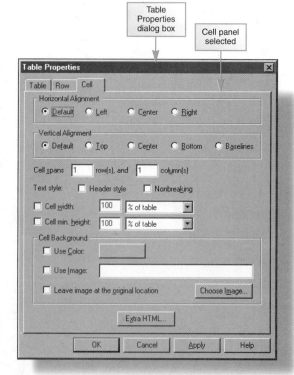

FIGURE 3-21

Cell properties include alignment, which is the position of text relative to the top, bottom, and sides of the selected cell. You can specify whether you want the selected cell to span more than one column or row. Clicking Header style will center the text in the selected cell and set its style to bold. Clicking Nonbreaking keeps the text from wrapping to the next line. Similarly to table width, you can set cell width as a percent of the table width or as a number of pixels. You also can set a background color or image for an individual cell.

A second table is used to contain the JobLinks page signature information. Unlike the first table you inserted, its borders are visible and its individual cell widths are not equal. Perform the following steps to insert a second table and set its cell properties.

Steps To Set Cell Properties

1 **Click below the table to move the insertion point to the first line below the table, press the ENTER key, and point to the Table button on the Composition toolbar.**

The insertion point is at the beginning of the second line below the first table. This is the location where the next table will be inserted (Figure 3-22).

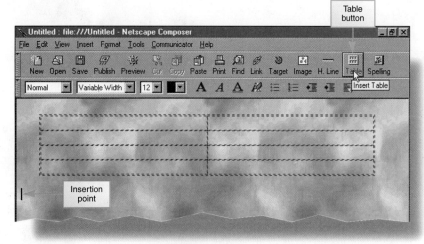

FIGURE 3-22

2 **Click the Table button. Type 3 in the Number of columns text box. Click Center in the Table Alignment area. Type 90 in the Table width text box. Point to the OK button.**

The new property values display as shown in Figure 3-23.

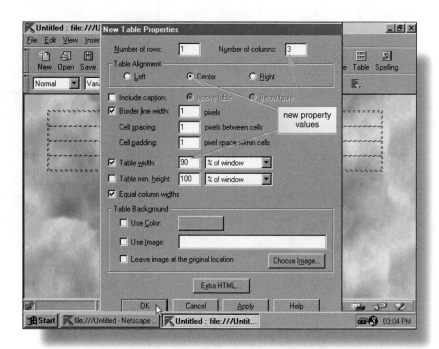

FIGURE 3-23

3 **Click the OK button. Right-click inside the leftmost cell in the second table and then point to Table Properties on the pop-up menu.**

The new table is added to the page. The pop-up menu displays (Figure 3-24).

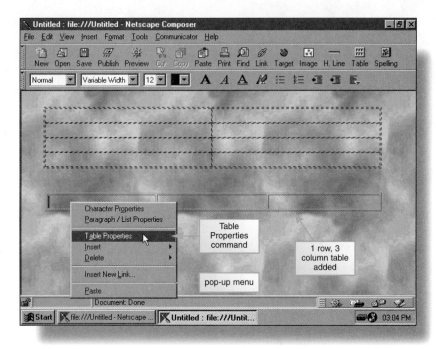

FIGURE 3-24

4 **Click Table Properties and then point to the Cell tab in the Table Properties dialog box.**

The Table Properties dialog box displays with the Table panel selected (Figure 3-25). The values on the Table panel are the ones you entered in the New Table Properties dialog box in Step 2.

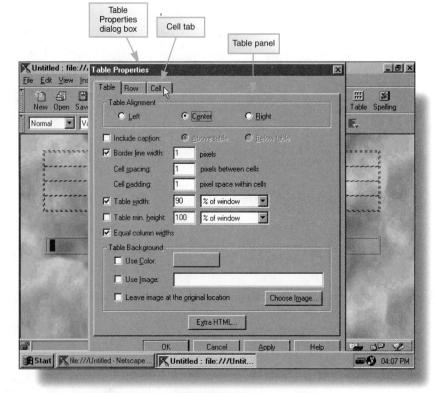

FIGURE 3-25

5 Click the Cell tab. Click Center in each of the two Alignment areas. Click Cell width and then type 25 in the Cell width text box.

The cell properties display as shown in Figure 3-26.

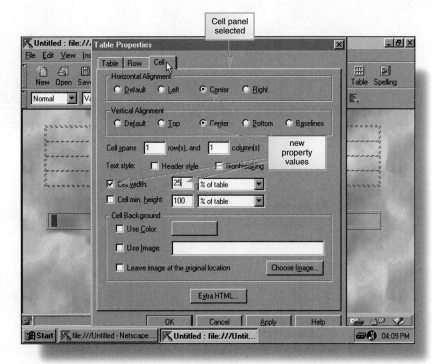

FIGURE 3-26

6 Click the OK button. Right-click inside the center cell of the lower table. Click Table Properties on the pop-up menu and then enter the cell properties shown in Figure 3-27.

The cell properties for the second cell display as shown in Figure 3-27.

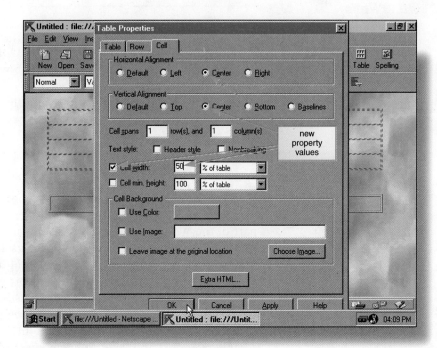

FIGURE 3-27

7 **Repeat Steps 3 through 5 for the rightmost cell in the table and then click the OK button.**

The table displays as shown in Figure 3-28. The insertion point displays in the center of the cell.

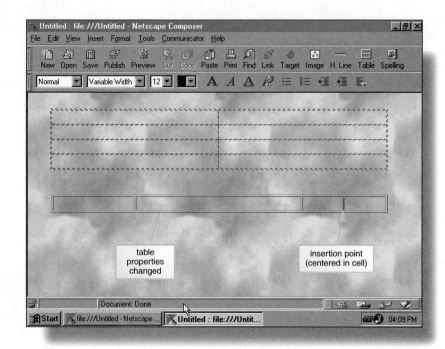

FIGURE 3-28

In the previous steps, you clicked the OK button in the Table Properties dialog box. The Table properties dialog box also contains an Apply/Close button. Clicking the OK button makes the changes and closes the dialog box. Clicking the Apply button previews the changes and then clicking the Close button accepts the changes and the dialog box closes.

Adding Inline Images

Recall from Project 1 that an **inline image** is a graphic or picture that appears as part of the Web page. Inline images are actually separate image files and are not contained within the HTML document itself. The images that you add to your Web page can be image files on your local disk or on a remote computer. Netscape and most of the current Web browsers support two image formats — GIF and JPEG. **GIF files** have a **.gif** extension and **JPEG files** have a **.jpg** extension. Composer also allows you to insert **bitmap graphic files (.bmp)** by converting them to JPEG format when you place them into your document.

Alternate text and **low-resolution images** are two extensions to displaying images in your Web page. Text-only browsers display alternate text instead of images. Both Navigator and Internet Explorer display alternate text as a pop-up bubble when the mouse pointer is over an image.

Low-resolution images are another alternate to normal image display. You specify a low-resolution image (smaller, faster loading file) to display first, while the normal image is still loading.

Inserting Images and Setting Image Properties

Depending on the settings you have specified in Composer Preferences, inserting an image in your Web page either copies the image file to the same directory as the Web page you are editing, or leaves the image file where it is. It is a good idea to have copies of the images under your control and in the same directory as the HTML document. That way you can be sure the image file will still be there every time the page is loaded in a browser.

You can use the items on the **Image panel** in the **Image Properties dialog box** (Figure 3-29) to insert a new image or change text wrapping, height and width, and spacing properties. If you do not want to have a copy of the image file placed in the same directory as the current document, you should click the Leave image at original location check box. The alignment buttons indicate the position of the selected image relative to text, as shown on the buttons. Not all alignment changes can be viewed in Composer. To see alignment changes you have made, preview your page in the browser.

In Bob's Job Links page, the list of links is presented as a bulleted list. The page does not, however, use the bullet list format. The bullets in this list actually are inline images. This is a common practice in Web pages because the HTML bullet styles are limited. Perform the following steps to insert an image for the bullet and set its properties.

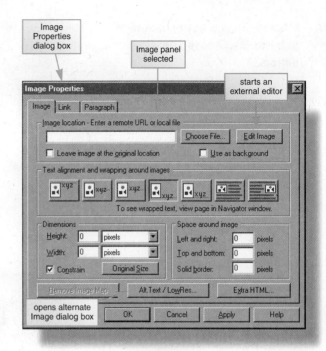

FIGURE 3-29

 Steps To Insert an Image and Set Image Properties

1 **Click the top-left cell of the top table and then point to the Image button on the Composition toolbar.**

The insertion point in the first cell is where the image will be inserted (Figure 3-30).

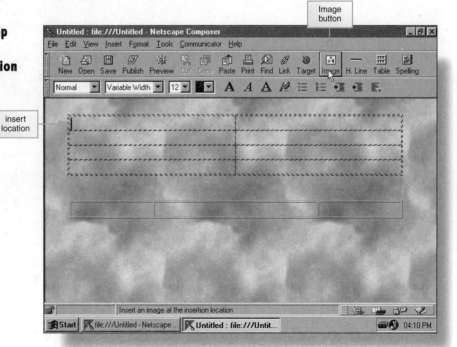

FIGURE 3-30

2 Click the Image button and then point to the Choose File button.

The Image Properties dialog box displays (Figure 3-31). If you know the location and name of the image file, you can type it in the Image location text box.

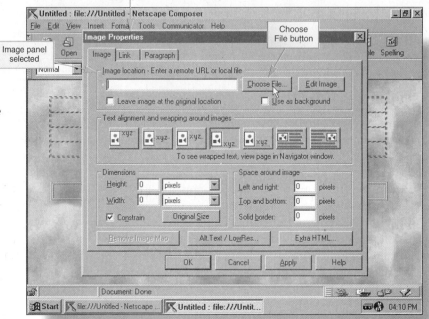

FIGURE 3-31

3 Click the Choose File button. When the Choose Image File dialog box displays, if necessary, click 3½ Floppy [A:] in the Look in list box, and then point to starbullet.gif (Figure 3-32).

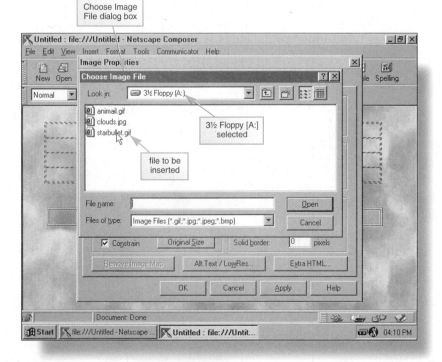

FIGURE 3-32

4 **Double-click starbullet.gif.**

The Choose Image File dialog box closes and the name of the selected file displays in the Image location text box (Figure 3-33).

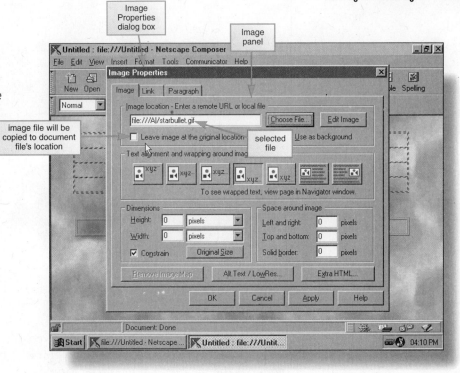

FIGURE 3-33

5 **Click the third alignment button from the left. Type 10 in the Top and bottom text box in the Space around image area. Point to the OK button.**

The new property settings display as shown in Figure 3-34.

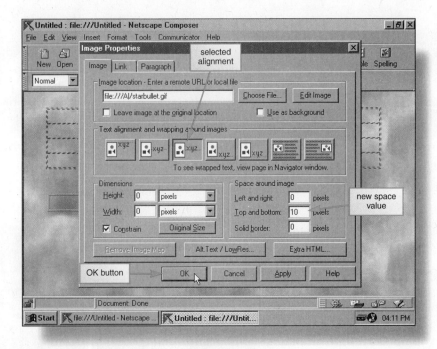

FIGURE 3-34

6 **Click the OK button.**

The image is inserted in the Web page (Figure 3-35).

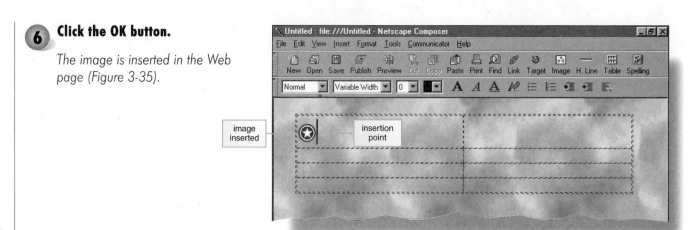

FIGURE 3-35

You can use Composer's Image Conversion dialog box when the image you want to add to your page is a bitmap graphics file (.bmp extension). Composer converts the file to the JPEG (.jpg) format, and allows you to select a high-, medium-, or low-quality pixel display.

Copying and Pasting Images

Netscape Composer provides drag and drop, cut, copy, and paste functions for you to manage image placement. In pages where the same image is used more than once, (such as the JobLinks bullets) it is much easier to paste copies of an image, rather than go through the insertion steps each time. Perform the following steps to copy the bullet image and paste it in the cells in the table.

 To Copy and Paste an Image

1 **Right-click the image and then point to Copy on the pop-up menu (Figure 3-36).**

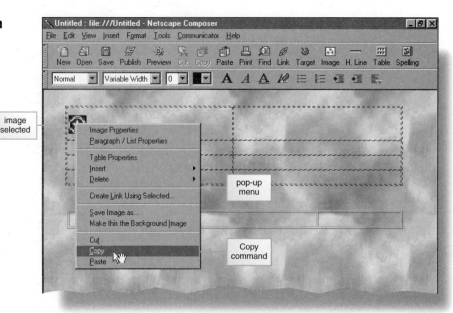

FIGURE 3-36

2 **Click Copy. Right-click inside the cell below the image and then point to Paste on the pop-up menu.**

The insertion point moves to the cell below the selected image and the pop-up menu displays (Figure 3-37).

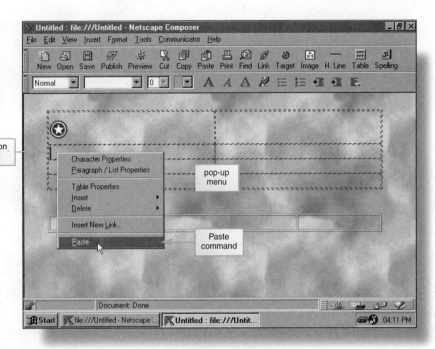

FIGURE 3-37

3 **Click Paste.**

The image is pasted to the new location. All of the image's properties also are copied (Figure 3-38).

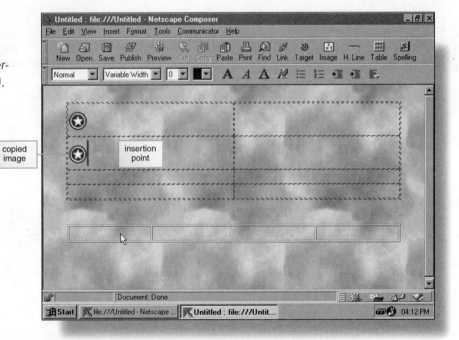

FIGURE 3-38

4 **Repeat Steps 2 and 3 six times to paste copies of the bullet image in each of the remaining cells.**

The table should displays as shown in Figure 3-39.

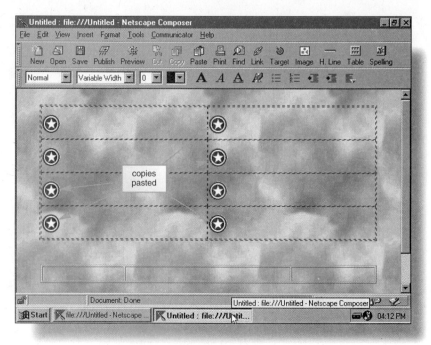

FIGURE 3-39

Other Ways

1. Click image to copy, press CTRL+C, click location where image is to appear, press CTRL+V

When you copy and paste an image, any properties you set for the image before it was copied will apply to the images that are pasted. You can see from the preceding steps that all copies of the bullet image have the same properties that you set for the first bullet image.

Formatting Text and Inserting Animated Images

In Project 2 , you learned how to edit text within Web pages and set character and paragraph properties. The JobLinks page contains text for the heading, links to other pages, and the page's signature information. Bob's page also uses an animated image as an email link. In the following steps, you first will enter and format the heading and link text and then you will enter and format the remaining text and insert the animated image.

Adding Heading Text and Link Text

Link text, also called **hypertext**, is the text that appears on a Web page that the reader can click to load another file into the browser. In the JobLinks page, each item in the two-column list provides a link to another Web site. In the next set of steps you will insert and format the text for these links. You will create the links themselves in a later step. Perform the following steps to insert and format the heading text and link text in the JobLinks page.

Steps To Insert and Format Text

1 Point to the upper-left corner of the edit area in the Composer window as shown in Figure 3-40.

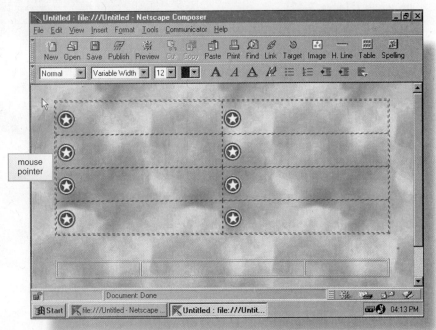

FIGURE 3-40

2 Click the mouse button. Press the ENTER key. Press the UP ARROW key. Type Bob's Job Links on the first line.

Two lines are inserted above the table and the text is inserted on the first line (Figure 3-41).

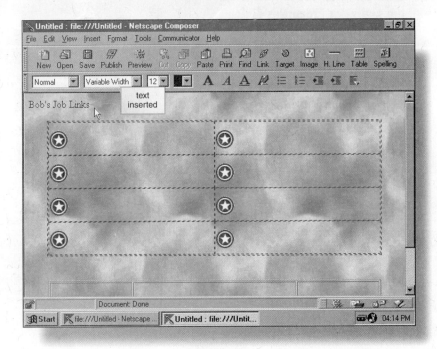

FIGURE 3-41

3 Select the text, right-click the selected text, and point to Character Properties on the pop-up menu (Figure 3-42).

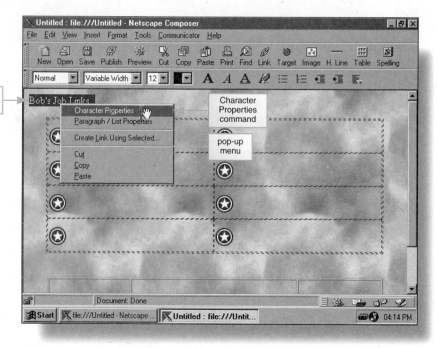

FIGURE 3-42

4 Click Character Properties. When the Character Properties dialog box displays, click the Use Color button in the Color area to display the color list box. Point to the color red (row 4, column 2) in the list box.

The Character Properties dialog box opens and the Character panel displays (Figure 3-43). On the Character panel, you can set various character formatting options.

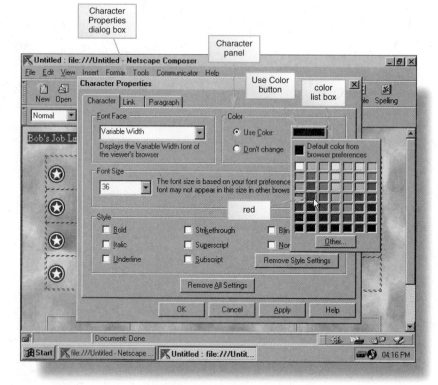

FIGURE 3-43

5 **Click the color red, click 36 in the Font Size list box, and point to the Paragraph tab.**

The new color and font size settings display on the Character panel (Figure 3-44).

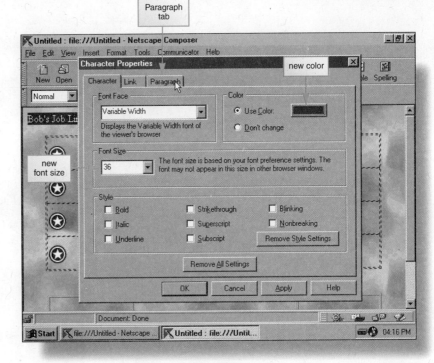

FIGURE 3-44

6 **Click the Paragraph tab. Click Center in the Alignment area on the Paragraph panel and then click the OK button.**

The new formatting features are applied to the selected text (Figure 3-45).

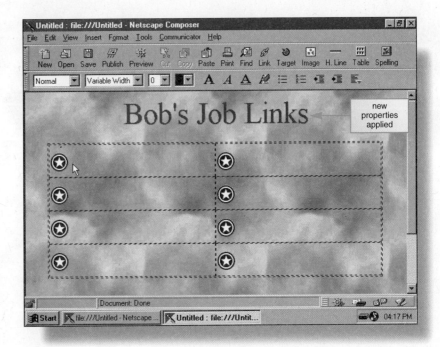

FIGURE 3-45

7 **Click to the right of the image in the top-left cell and then type** TOPjobs **in the first cell.**

The text is inserted (Figure 3-46).

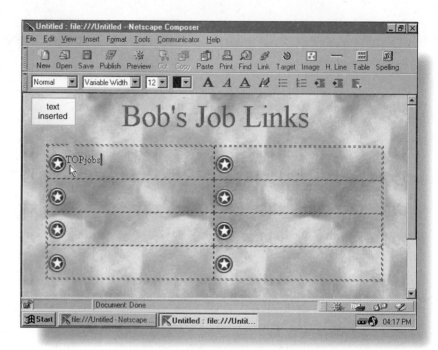

FIGURE 3-46

8 **Repeat Step 6 seven times to insert the remaining text that will serve as links to other pages.**

The inserted text displays as shown in Figure 3-47.

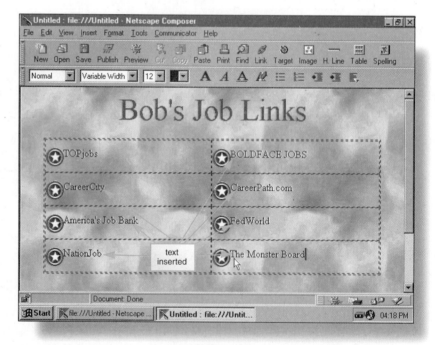

FIGURE 3-47

Formatting Text and Inserting an Animated Image

In this next set of steps, you will add and format the text that serves as the signature of the page. Also, you will insert the animated image that will serve as the email link.

When you are entering text and you press the ENTER key, Composer inserts a **new paragraph tag**, which causes a blank line to be inserted on the page. If you want text to continue to the line immediately below the line you are typing, you must insert a **line break** by pressing the CTRL+SHIFT keys.

Animated GIF files are image files in the GIF format that have a short series of different images displayed in succession in the same location, giving the appearance of motion. Many animated GIF files for Web pages are available in clip art libraries. Perform the following steps to complete the text for the JobLinks page and insert the animated mail image.

More *About*
Animated GIF Files

For more information on how animated GIF images work and how you can create your own animated GIF files, visit the Composer Web site (www.scsite.com/nc/pr3.htm) and click the link to Animated GIF.

 Steps **To Format Text and Insert an Animated Image**

1 **Click the left cell in the lower table. Type** Bob's Job Links **and then press the** SHIFT+ENTER **keys. Type** is maintained by **and then press the** SHIFT+ENTER **keys. Type** Bob Davis **as the last line.**

The text with line breaks displays as shown in Figure 3-48.

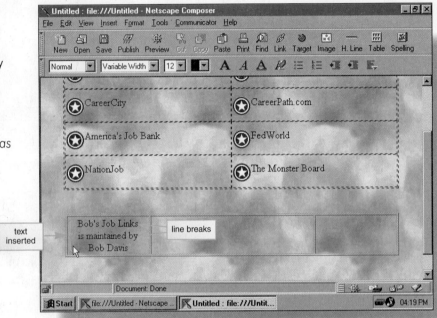

FIGURE 3-48

2 **Select the text in the left cell. Click the Italic button on the Formatting toolbar. Press the** RIGHT ARROW **key two times.**

The formatted text displays as shown in Figure 3-49. The insertion point displays in the center cell.

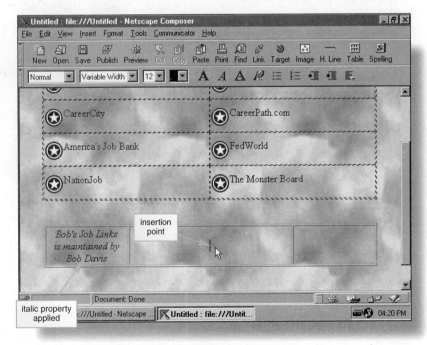

FIGURE 3-49

3 Type the text without line breaks as shown in Figure 3-50.

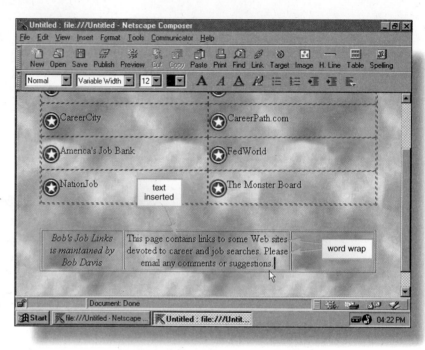

FIGURE 3-50

4 Select the text in the center cell. Apply the following formatting using the Formatting toolbar. Click the Bold button, click 12 in the Font Size list box, and click the color red (row 4, column 2) in the Font Color list box. Press the RIGHT ARROW key two times and then point to the Image button on the Composition toolbar.

The text in the lower table displays as shown in Figure 3-51.

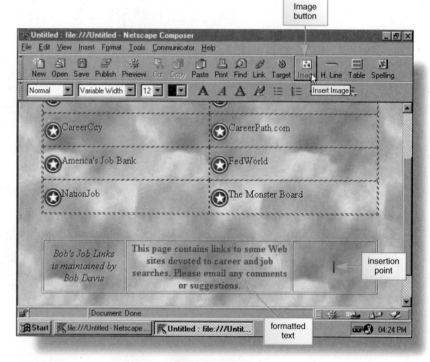

FIGURE 3-51

5 Click the Image button, click the Choose File button, and point to animail.gif.

Both the Image Properties and Choose Image File dialog boxes are open (Figure 3-52).

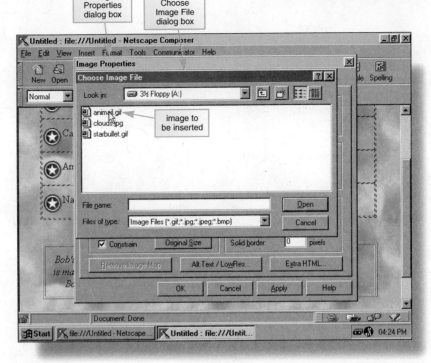

FIGURE 3-52

6 Double-click animail.gif and then click the OK button.

The animated image is added to the page (Figure 3-53).

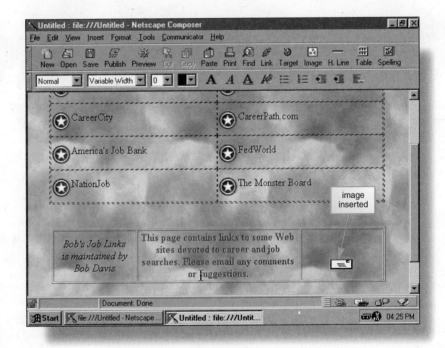

FIGURE 3-53

7 **Press the SHIFT+ENTER keys. Type** bob@email.oku.edu **and then select the email address text. Click the Italic button on the Formatting toolbar.**

The email address displays in italics below the animated image (Figure 3-54).

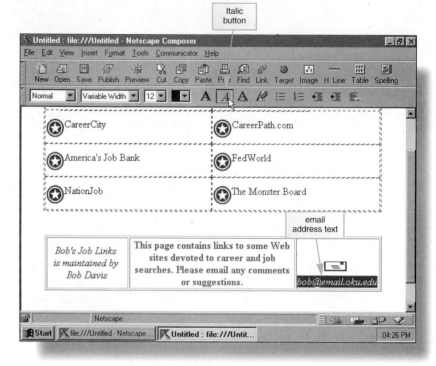

FIGURE 3-54

8 **Select all of the text in the table of links and then apply bold and font size 18.**

The text in the links table displays as shown in Figure 3-55.

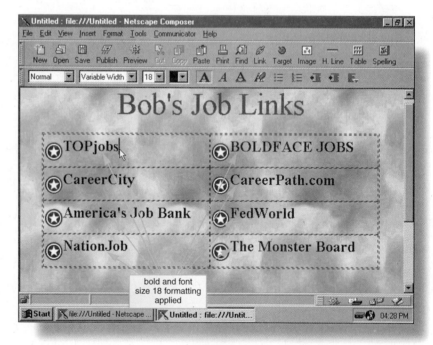

FIGURE 3-55

If the document you're editing contains an animated GIF file, it can become distracting pretty quickly. You can press the ESC key to keep it from continually loading while you edit the document.

Linking Text and Images to Other Web Pages

You can use text links and image links to produce words, sounds, pictures, or even action video on your own computer. This is accomplished by **linking** the text or image to some other file. Just as with text, you can have images that behave as links in your documents. When you click a linked image, the Navigator window displays the page that the image is linked to.

You can set link properties on the **Link panel** in the **Image Properties dialog box** (Figure 3-56) or the Link panel in the **Character Properties dialog box** (both Link panels are similar). Use the settings on the Link panel to insert a new link or modify an existing link's properties.

In the Enter text to display for a new link text box, you enter the text you want to create a new link to. If you have already selected an image or text in your page to link to, it automatically displays in the text box. In the Link to page location or local file text box, you can type a URL directly or you can click the Choose File button to select a file. You should recall that you used the Select a named target list box to create the links to targets in the catering page in Project 2.

The hypertext and corresponding URLs for the JobLinks page are listed in Table 3-1.

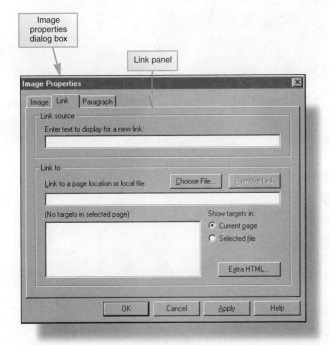

FIGURE 3-56

Table 3-1	
LINK	URL
TOPjobs	http://www.topjobsusa.com
CareerCity	http://www.adamsonline.com
America's Job Bank	http://www.ajb.dni.us
NationJob	http://www.nationjob.com
BOLDFACE JOBS	http://www.boldfacejobs.com
CareerPath.com	http://www.careerpath.com
FedWorld	http://www.fedworld.gov/jobs/jobsearch.html
The Monster Board	http://www.monster.com

Bob's page contains eight text links (one to each of the Web sites) and one image link (to an email address). Complete the steps on the next page to create these links using selected text and images.

Steps To Create a Link with Selected Text and Images

1 **Select the TOPjobs text. Right-click the selected text and then point to Create Link Using Selected on the pop-up menu.**

The TOPjobs text is selected and the pop-up menu displays (Figure 3-57).

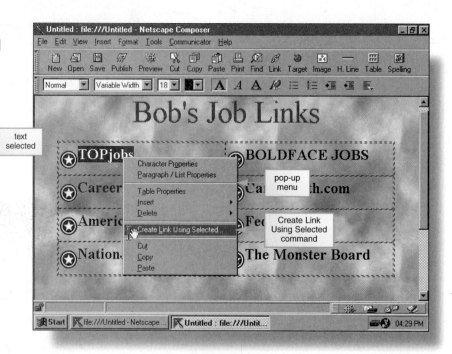

FIGURE 3-57

2 **Click Create Link Using Selected. Type** http://www. topjobsusa.com **in the Link to a page location or local file text box and then point to the OK button.**

The URL displays on the Link panel in the Character Properties dialog box (Figure 3-58).

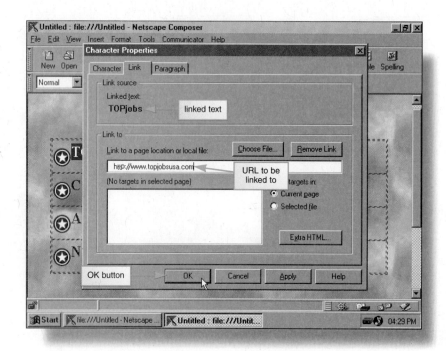

FIGURE 3-58

3 **Click the OK button.**

The text is underlined and is assigned the blue link text color set in Preferences (Figure 3-59).

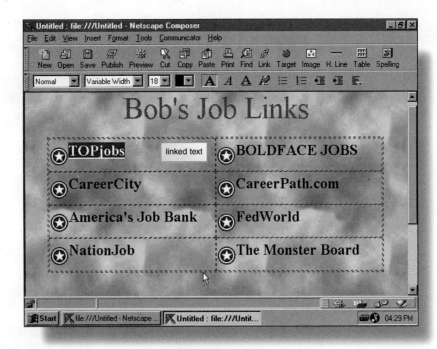

FIGURE 3-59

4 **Repeat Steps 1 through 4 for the remaining links, using the URLs in Table 3-1 on page NC 3.33.**

The Bob's Job Links table is complete (Figure 3-60).

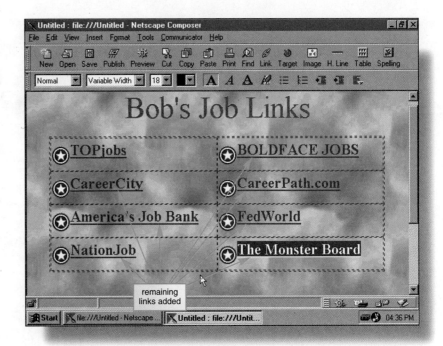

FIGURE 3-60

5 Right-click the animated email image, click Create Link Using Selected on the pop-up menu, and type `mailto:bob@email.oku.edu` in the Link to a page location or local file text box. Point to the OK button.

The mailto URL displays in the Link to text box (Figure 3-61).

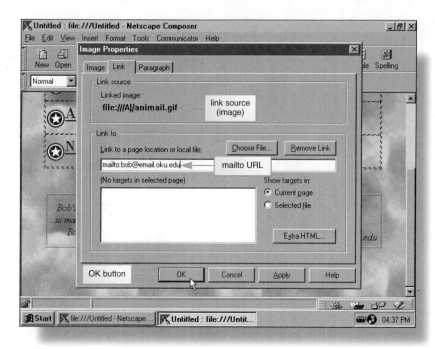

FIGURE 3-61

6 Click the OK button and then point to the mail image.

The URL linked to displays on the status bar when the mouse pointer is positioned on the image (Figure 62).

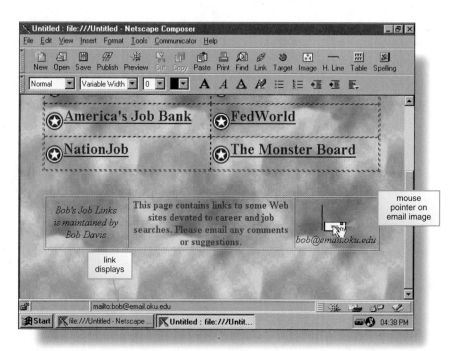

FIGURE 3-62

Many variations and extensions are possible with link tags in HTML that Composer does not support directly. You can, however, click the Extra HTML button on the Link panel to display a dialog box in which you can add other HTML or JavaScript to the link tag.

Saving the JobLinks Page

Before continuing, it is always a good idea to save your work. Complete the following steps to save the JobLinks page on a floppy disk in drive A.

TO SAVE THE JOBLINKS PAGE

① Click the Save button on the Composition toolbar. If necessary, click 3½ Floppy [A:] in the Save in list box and then type JobLinks in the File name text box.

② Click the Save button in the Save As dialog box.

The Save As dialog displays as shown in Figure 3-63 before clicking the OK button. When you click the OK button, the file is saved with the file name, JobLinks.

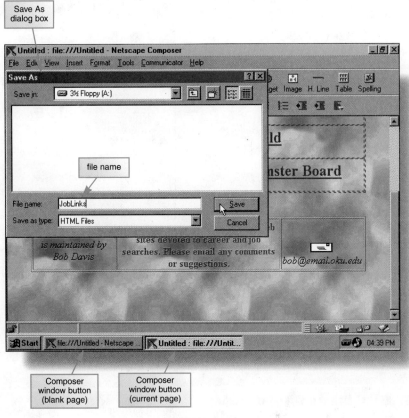

FIGURE 3-63

Dragging and Dropping Images and Changing Image Properties

In previous steps, you inserted a local graphics file (starbullet) into the JobLinks page using the Image Properties dialog box. You also can drag and drop any image from a Navigator or Composer window into your document. When you add an image to a page you are not limited to using its original size. In the next sets of steps, you will drag and drop an image and then change its size on the page and other properties.

Dragging and Dropping Images

Perform the steps on the next page to drag and drop a horizontal rule image from another Web page onto the JobLinks page.

Steps **To Drag and Drop an Image**

1 Close the Composer window with the blank page. Click the Navigator icon on the Component bar and then type
`home.netscape.com/assist/ net_sites/starter/samples/ rules.html` **in the Netsite text box. Press the ENTER key.**

The Netscape Rules and Bullets Web page displays in the browser (Figure 3-64). You also can obtain the horizontal rule image from www.scsite.com/nc/pr3.htm.

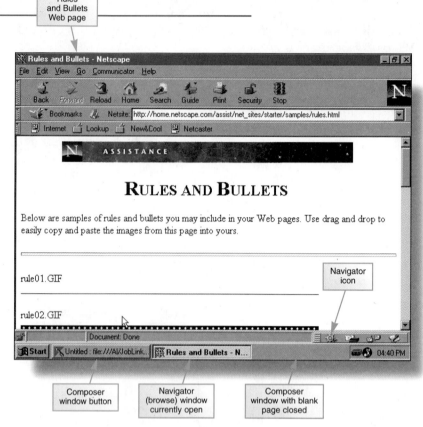

FIGURE 3-64

2 Right-click the Windows taskbar and then point to Tile Vertically on the pop-up menu.

The pop-up menu displays (Figure 3-65).

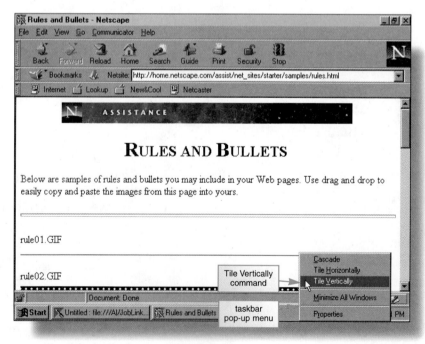

FIGURE 3-65

3 Click Tile Vertically and then click the blank line above the links table in the Composer window.

The Navigator and Composer windows display side by side (Figure 3-66).

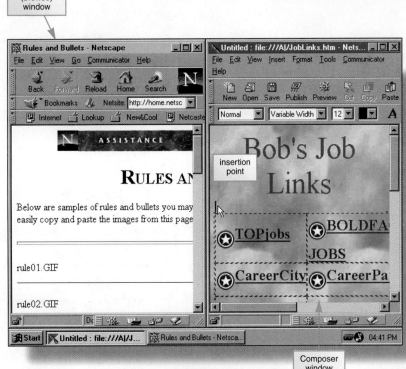

FIGURE 3-66

4 Scroll down the page in the Navigator window and then point to rule11.GIF.

The Navigator window scrolls independently from the Composer window (Figure 3-67).

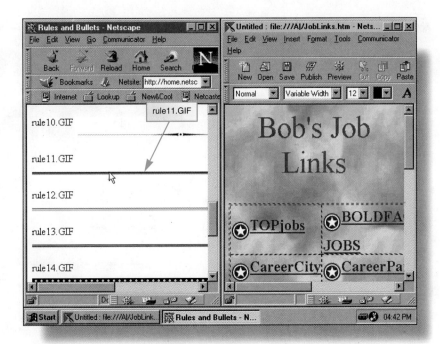

FIGURE 3-67

5 **Drag rule 11.GIF to the position shown in Figure 3-68.**

The mouse pointer changes to an image icon (Figure 3-68).

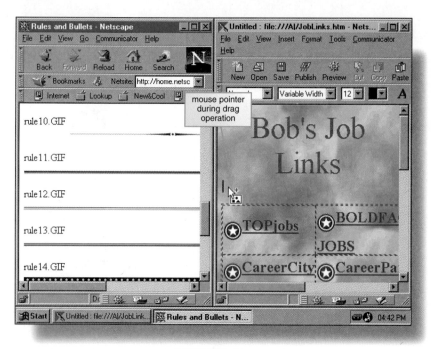

FIGURE 3-68

6 **Drop the image by releasing the mouse button.**

The image is added to the page (Figure 3-69).

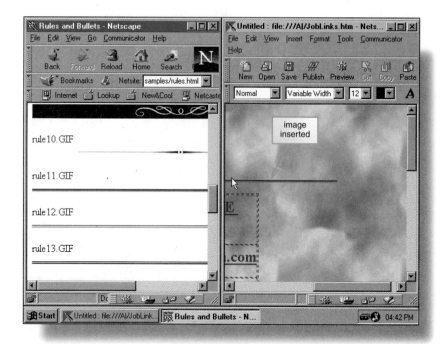

FIGURE 3-69

You also can drag and drop hyperlinks from the bookmark, mail news, or browse windows.

Changing an Image's Properties

In previous steps, you linked the animated mail image by working with the Link panel in the Image Properties dialog. The Image Properties dialog box has two additional panels you can use to set image properties — the **Image panel** and the **Paragraph panel**.

In the Dimensions area on the Image panel, you can set the height and width of the image in pixels. If you check the Constrain box, changing either height or width will automatically make a proportional change to the other dimension. You can change the image's alignment on the page on the Paragraph panel. Perform the following steps to increase the height of the horizontal line image and center it on the JobLinks page.

 Steps **To Set an Image's Properties**

1 Close the Navigator window, maximize the Composer window, right-click the line image, and point to Image Properties on the pop-up menu.

The pop-up menu displays (Figure 3-70).

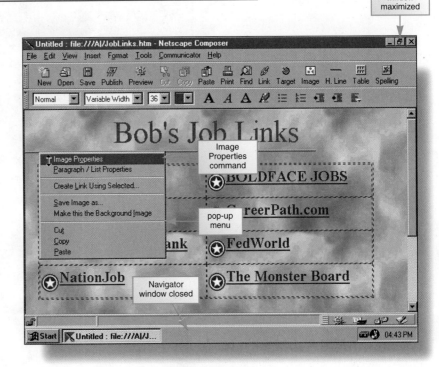

FIGURE 3-70

2 Click Image Properties. When the Image Properties dialog box displays, click Constrain to deselect the check box and then type 8 in the Height text box in the Dimensions area. Point to the Paragraph tab.

The new settings display as shown in Figure 3-71.

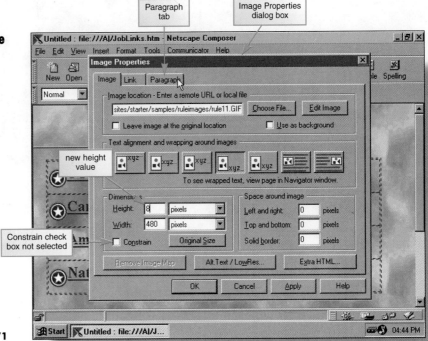

FIGURE 3-71

3 **Click the Paragraph tab, click Center in the Alignment area and point to the OK button.**

The new alignment setting displays (Figure 3-72).

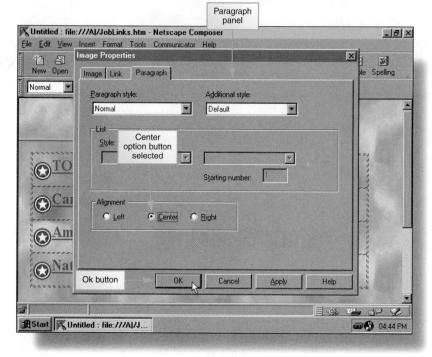

FIGURE 3-72

4 **Click the OK button.**

The centered, resized horizontal line image displays as shown in Figure 3-73.

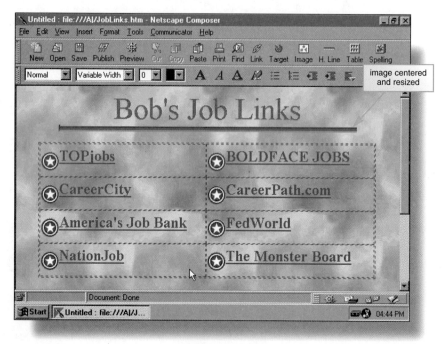

FIGURE 3-73

Once you have inserted an image, you can resize it by selecting it and then dragging the handles at each corner. Click Edit Image to edit the image file using the external image editor you specified in the General panel in the Composer Preferences dialog box.

JavaScript and HTML Tags

JavaScript is a programming language that you can use with Composer to add functionality to your Web pages by transferring some of the processing tasks from the Web **server** (remote host) to the **client** (local PC running Netscape). A JavaScript is a stored set of instructions — a program. Instead of being stored as a separate file, however, the JavaScript code is included as part of a standard HTML document.

In this project, you will insert a simple JavaScript statement into the JobLinks Web page that causes the current date and time to be displayed on the page every time it is loaded. JavaScript statements are contained in an HTML document within the **<script>** and **</script>** tags. JavaScripts can be very complex and sophisticated. Numerous books devoted entirely to using JavaScript in Web pages are available.

Composer does not support some HTML tags directly. These include tags for forms, JavaScript, and image maps. Composer does, however, provide a special **tag icon** that you can use to insert raw HTML into your page. Perform the following steps to insert HTML script tags and a JavaScript statement.

More *About*
JavaScript

JavaScript is not the same as Java. Java is a more powerful (and complex) language for creating Web applications called applets. For more information on the differences between Java and JavaScript, visit the Composer Web site (www.scsite.com/nc/pr3.htm) and click the link to Java.

 Steps **To Insert HTML Tags and JavaScript**

---

1 **Click to the right of the s in Links and then press the ENTER key. Click the Remove All Styles button on the Formatting toolbar.**

A blank line is inserted with an insertion point (Figure 3-74).

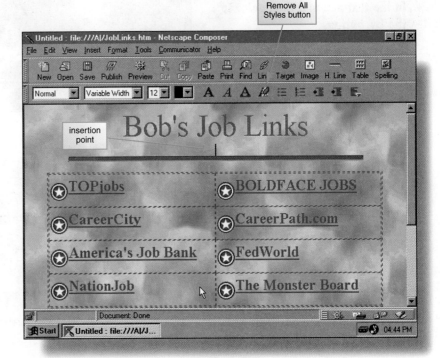

FIGURE 3-74

2 Click Insert on the menu bar and then point to HTML Tag.

The Insert menu displays (Figure 3-75).

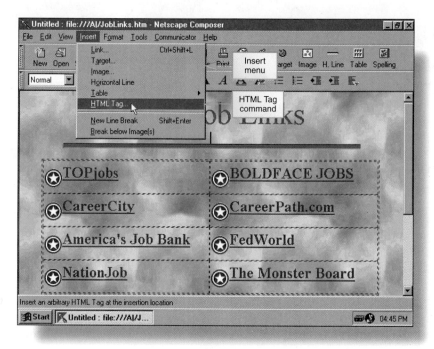

FIGURE 3-75

3 Click HTML Tag. Type `<script>` in the text box and then point to the OK button.

The HTML Tag dialog box displays (Figure 3-76).

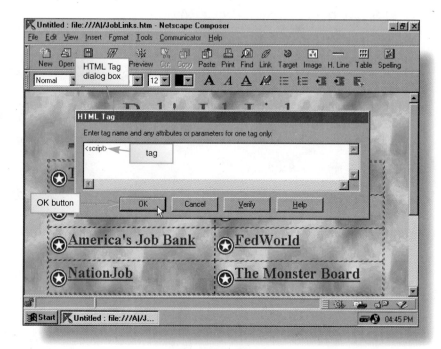

FIGURE 3-76

4 **Click the OK button and then type** `document.write(Date())`. **Click Insert on the menu bar and then point to HTML Tag.**

A tag icon is inserted and the text you typed follows the tag (Figure 3-77).

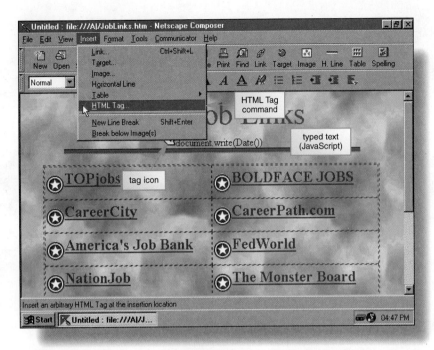

FIGURE 3-77

5 **Click HTML Tag. Type** `</script>` **in the text box and then point to the OK button.**

The close script tag displays in the text box (Figure 3-78).

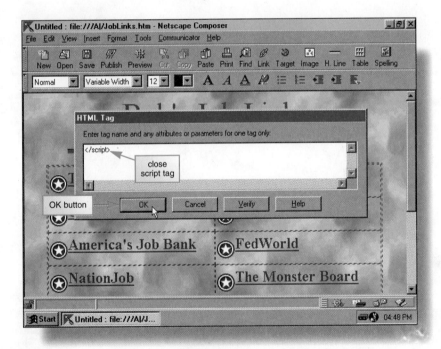

FIGURE 3-78

6 **Click the OK button, and then point to the Preview button on the Composition toolbar.**

A tag icon for the second tag is inserted (Figure 3-79).

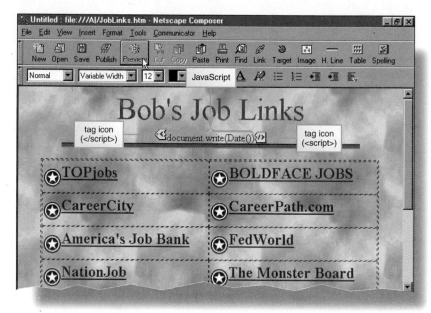

FIGURE 3-79

Other Ways

1. Press ALT+I, press H

Many pages that use sophisticated JavaScripts contain functions and sub-routines written with JavaScript. It is customary to include these scripts within the head section of the HTML document. Although Composer allows you to add JavaScript, you can insert it only within the body section of the HTML document. For this reason, you may need to return to a text editor with your Composer-created page to do advanced HTML programming and scripting.

Saving and Testing a Web Page

Bob's Job Links page is complete. Perform the following steps to save and test the Web page.

Steps **To Save and Test a Web Page**

1 **Click the Preview button and then point to the Yes button.**

The Netscape dialog box displays (Figure 3-80).

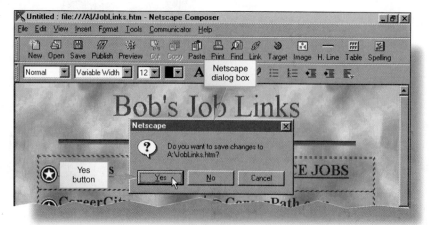

FIGURE 3-80

2 **Click the Yes button.**

The JobLinks page displays in a Netscape browse window (Figure 3-81).

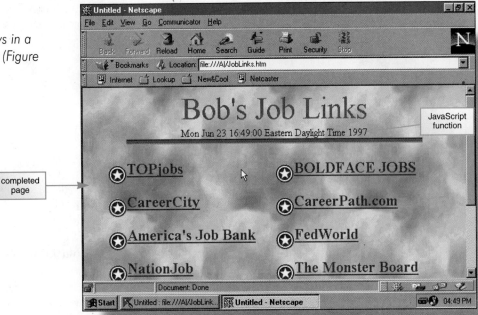

FIGURE 3-81

3 **Test the links from the browse window and then click the Composer icon on the Component bar. Point to the Publish button on the Composition toolbar.**

The browse window is still open on the desktop (Figure 3-82).

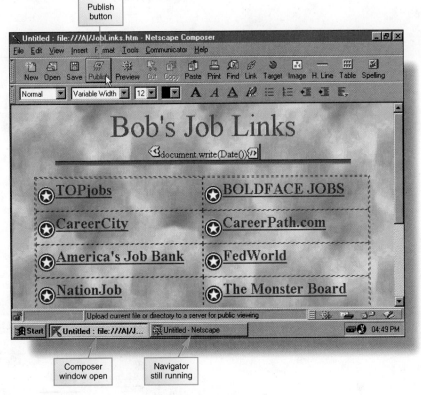

FIGURE 3-82

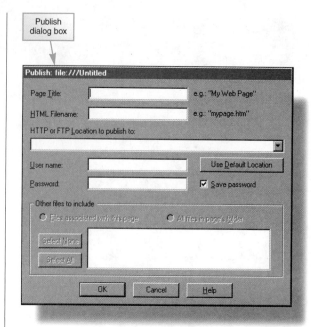

FIGURE 3-83

If any link does not work properly, check to be sure that you entered the correct URL when you made the link. You can edit or modify the link by selecting the link text and then clicking the Link button on the Composition toolbar.

Publishing a Web Page

If you have access to a Web server, Netscape Composer provides an easy way to publish your documents on the Internet. **Publishing** a Web page is the process of sending copies of page files to a server where they are then available to the World Wide Web. Composer allows you to click a single button to publish your Web page by entering information in the Publish dialog box (Figure 3-83). If you have access to a Web server, you can perform the following steps to Publish the JobLinks page.

 To Publish a Web Page

1 **Click the Publish button. Type a title and location to publish to and then point to the OK button.**

All image files will be transferred with the Web page (Figure 3-84).

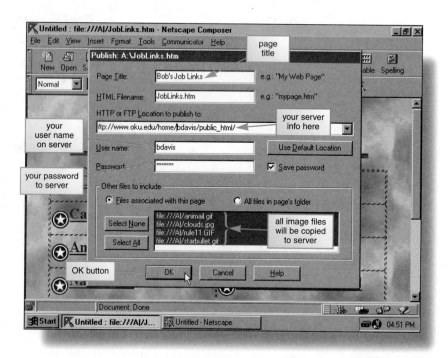

2 **Click the OK button and then point to the Continue button in the Security Information dialog box, if it displays.**

You can disable the display of the Security Information dialog box by clicking the check box (Figure 3-85).

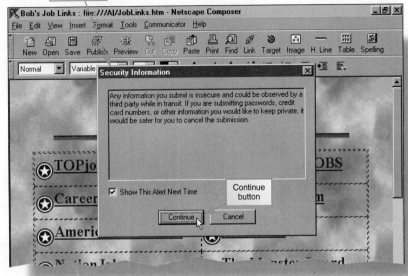

FIGURE 3-85

3 **If the dialog box displays, click the Continue button. Point to the OK button in the Netscape dialog box.**

The Netscape dialog box displays stating that all files were uploaded successfully (Figure 3-86).

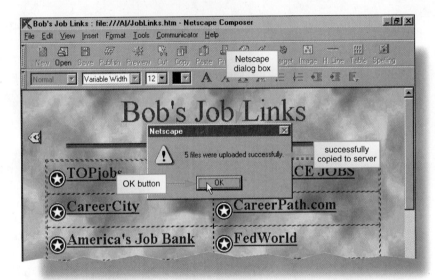

FIGURE 3-86

4 **Click the OK button and then point to the script tag icon.**

Composer may combine the two tag icons with the JavaScript. You can view the contents of a tag icon by pointing to it (Figure 3-87).

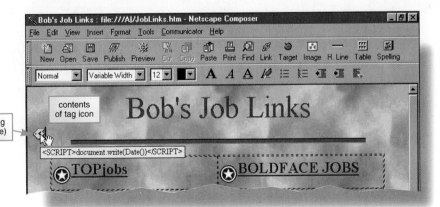

FIGURE 3-87

The display of the page in the browser is the preview of the local file for the JobLinks page. For a final test, enter the URL that you gave for the JobLinks page when you uploaded it to the server and test the page and its links.

Quitting Communicator

The project is complete. Perform the following steps to quit Netscape Communicator.

TO QUIT COMMUNICATOR

1 Click the Composer window's Close button.
2 Click the Navigator browse window's Close button.

Project Summary

Project 2 introduced you to basic text editing within a Web page. Project 3 introduced you to more sophisticated features such as creating a page texture, using tables, inserting and editing images, and creating hyperlinks from text and images. You learned more ways to interact with Composer through its various property dialog boxes. You learned how to use the drag and drop capability of Composer. You learned about JavaScript. You created a Web page from a blank document, saved it, tested it, and published it on the World Wide Web.

What You Should Know

Having completed this project, you now should be able to perform the following tasks:

- Copy and Paste an Image *(NC 3.22)*
- Create a Link with Selected Text and Images *(NC 3.34)*
- Download Image Files *(NC 3.7)*
- Drag and Drop an Image *(NC 3.38)*
- Format Text and Insert an Animated Image *(NC 3.37)*
- Insert a Table and Set Table Properties *(NC 3.13)*
- Insert an Image and Set Image Properties *(NC 3.19)*
- Insert and Format Text *(NC 3.25)*

- Insert HTML Tags and JavaScript *(NC 3.43)*
- Open a Composer Window with a Blank Page *(NC 3.7)*
- Publish a Web Page *(NC 3.48)*
- Quit Communicator *(NC 3.50)*
- Save and Test a Web Page *(NC 3.46)*
- Save the JobLinks Page *(NC 3.37)*
- Set an Image's Properties *(NC 3.41)*
- Set Cell Properties *(NC 3.15)*
- Set Page Properties *(NC 3.9)*

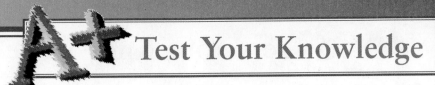

Test Your Knowledge

1 True/False

Instructions: Circle T if the statement is true or F if the statement is false.

T F 1. A Web page will always display the same in different browsers.

T F 2. Clip art images are never copyrighted.

T F 3. Text links always appear in blue.

T F 4. A small image is tiled to create a texture.

T F 5. Most Web search engines locate pages by their keywords.

T F 6. A table with a border width equal to zero does not display in Composer.

T F 7. A table can be inserted in a cell of another table.

T F 8. Individual cells in a table can have background colors and images.

T F 9. Individual columns in a table can have background colors and images.

T F 10. You can drag and drop images only from another Composer window.

2 Multiple Choice

Instructions: Circle the correct response.

1. Which of the following is not a font property available in Composer?
   a. fixed width
   b. superscript
   c. strikeout
   d. blinking

2. Each _____ on a page can have a different background color or texture.
   a. table
   b. table row
   c. table cell
   d. all of the above

3. You can drag an image from a _____ window and drop it in a Composer window.
   a. Composer
   b. Navigator
   c. both a and b
   d. neither a nor b

4. When you start Composer from the Windows Start menu, a Composer window containing a _____ is opened on the desktop.
   a. home page
   b. template
   c. page wizard
   d. blank page

(continued)

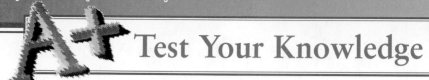

Test Your Knowledge

Multiple Choice *(continued)*

5. Of the following, which Web page feature cannot be accomplished with Composer?
   a. frames
   b. tables
   c. JavaScripts
   d. HTML tags

6. Of the following, which will not display in a Composer window?
   a. zero width table borders
   b. HTML tag icons
   c. text wrap around images
   d. none of the above

7. To maintain an image's proportions when changing either height or width, the _____ check box on the Image panel should be checked.
   a. Expand
   b. Constrain
   c. Proportional
   d. none of the above

8. Of the following, which is not an Image Properties dialog box tabbed panel?
   a. Image
   b. Link
   c. Character
   d. Paragraph

9. Of the following table properties, which one cannot be set in the Table Properties dialog box?
   a. alignment
   b. number of columns
   c. border width
   d. cell width

10. Alternatives to normal image display include _____.
    a. low-resolution images
    b. alternate text
    c. both a and b
    d. neither a nor b

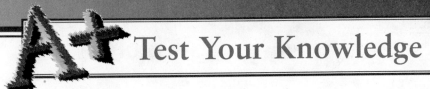

Test Your Knowledge

3 Understanding the Image Properties Dialog Box

Instructions: In Figure 3-88, arrows point to several controls on the Image panel in the Image Properties dialog box. In the spaces provided, briefly explain the function of each control.

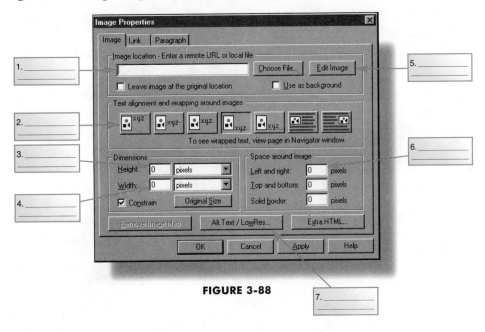

FIGURE 3-88

4 Understanding the Page Properties Dialog Box

Instructions: In Figure 3-89, arrows point to several controls on the Colors and Background panel in the Page Properties dialog box. In the spaces provided, briefly explain the function of each control.

FIGURE 3-89

Use Help

1 Using Netscape Help

Instructions: Start Netscape Composer, and perform the following tasks with a computer.

1. Click Help on the menu bar and then click Help Contents.
2. Click Composing and editing Web pages.
3. Click the Find button in the Help window (Figure 3-90).
4. Type edit dictionary dialog box in the Find what text box and then click the Find Next button.
5. What is the function of the Edit Dictionary dialog box?
6. Print your answer and turn it in to your instructor.

Find button

FIGURE 3-90

Use Help

2 Online Product Information and Support

Instructions: Start Netscape Composer and perform the following tasks with a computer.

1. Click Help on the menu bar and then click Product Information and Support.
2. Scroll down the page (Figure 3-91) to the Other Useful Information section and click Other Useful Links.
3. Scroll down the page to the Creating Web Pages section.
4. Click any one of the links under the Creating Web Pages category.
5. Explore the page.
6. Write a brief summary of what you found and turn it in to your instructor.

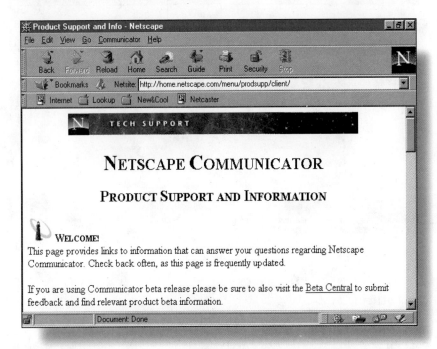

FIGURE 3-91

Apply Your Knowledge

1 Setting Image and Table Properties

Instructions: Figure 3-92 shows the Apply Your Knowledge Web Page as it should display in the Netscape browser. Apply-3 is a file containing all of the elements in this page, but without the correct image and table property settings.

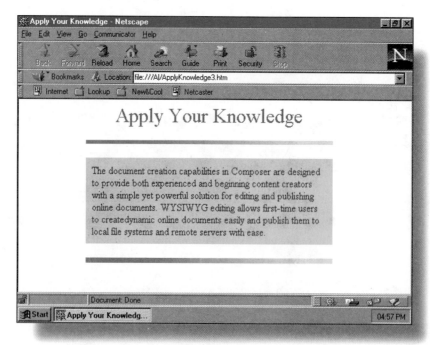

FIGURE 3-92

Perform the following activities.

1. Start Composer.
2. Open the file Apply-3 from the Composer Web site at www.scsite.com/nc/pr3.htm.
3. Make changes to only the image and table properties for the page to display in a browse window as shown in Figure 3-92.
4. Save the file, giving it the name, ApplyKnowledge3.
5. Print the revised document.
6. Write your name on the printout and hand it in to your instructor.

In the Lab

1 Working with Background Colors and Images

Problem: You have decided to give Bob's Job Links a different look (Figure 3-93). You want to keep the content and layout, but give the page a different background arrangement.

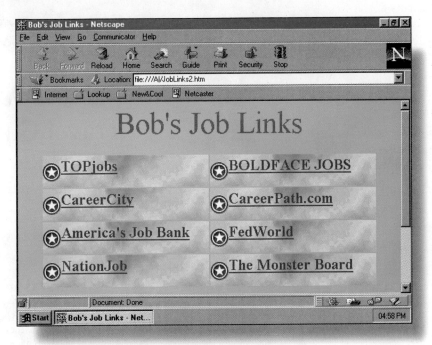

FIGURE 3-93

Instructions: Perform the following tasks.

1. Start Composer and open the JobLinks page you created in this project.
2. Delete the JavaScript and the two horizontal line images.
3. Click Format on the menu bar and then click Page Colors and Properties.
4. Click Use Image to deselect it, click the Background button, and click the color blue (row 3 column 6). Click the OK button.
5. Right-click the table of job links and then click Table Properties on the pop-up menu.
6. Click Use Image, click the Choose Image button, double-click clouds.jpg, and click the OK button.
7. Repeat Step 5 and Step 6 for the signature information table.
8. Click File on the menu bar and then click Save As. Save the file as JobLinks2.
9. Preview the page and print it from the Navigator window.
10. Write your name on the printout and hand it in to your instructor.

In the Lab

2 Controlling Page Layout with Tables

Problem: The Far and Away Travel Club wants a more dynamic layout for its current Web page (Figure 3-94).

Instructions: Perform the following tasks.

1. Open the Travel Club page in Composer. (travel.htm is available from Netscape's Templates page and from www.scsite.com/nc/pr3.htm).

2. Delete the template information at the top of the page.

3. Insert a 3 row, 2 column table with border width = 0, and center alignment.

4. Select the club's logo image. Cut and paste the image into the top-left cell. Set the horizontal alignment property for only this cell equal to Center.

FIGURE 3-94

5. Select the title text. Cut and paste the title into the top-right cell.

6. Select the Rare Trips heading and paragraph. Cut and paste the text into the center row, left cell.

7. Select the entire section at the bottom of the page containing the list of links and their bullet images. Cut and paste the text into the center row, right cell.

8. Cut and paste the Aztec Temple image into the bottom-left cell.

9. Cut and paste the Special Sojourn section into the bottom-right cell.

10. Delete the remaining text, rules, and images below the table.

11. Save the page as Travel2 and print the page.

12. Write your name on the printout and turn it in to your instructor.

In the Lab

3 Dissecting Web Pages

Problem: You want to sharpen your skills at finding out how good looking Web pages are laid out so you can apply this knowledge to your own pages.

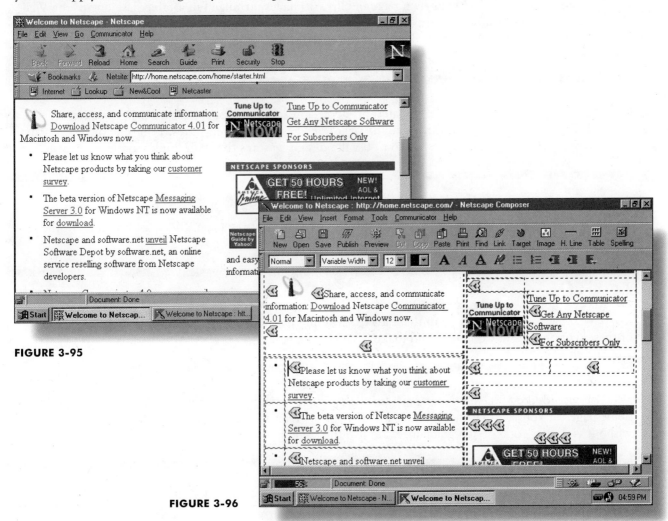

FIGURE 3-95

FIGURE 3-96

Instructions: Perform the following tasks.

1. Start Navigator. Browse the Web until you find a Web page with an attractive, multicolumn layout, but no visible table borders.
2. Open the page in Composer.
3. If you do not see the dotted outline of a table on the page, keep browsing the Web until you find one.
4. Print the Web page.
5. On the printout, draw the table borders.
6. Write your name on the printout of the page and turn it in to your instructor.

Cases and Places

The difficulty of these case studies varies: ❱ are the least difficult; ❱❱ are more difficult; and ❱❱❱ are the most difficult.

1 ❱ You would like to create your own page of clip art images, arranged in a table. Use one of the Web search engines to find sources of free Web page clip art. Drag and drop at least nine clip art images that you like best onto your own page. Add a heading and signature section to the page. Publish the page if you have access to a Web server.

2 ❱ Many companies that offer Web-related products and services sponsor award programs for Web pages. Search for one of these award-winning pages or "best of the Web" sites. Print one of the award-winning pages. On the back of the printout, list the design features that you think won it an award.

3 ❱ The White House has contracted you to redesign its home page (www.whitehouse.gov). Keep the same content, but redesign the background, colors, and layout of the page. Make a local copy of the file, but do not publish it.

4 ❱❱ Many companies that offer Web-related products and services sponsor award programs for the *worst* Web pages. Search for one of these award-winning pages or "worst of the Web" sites. Open one of these worst pages in Composer and make it one of the best.

5 ❱❱❱ You would like to have a home page (or make improvements if you already have one). Create a home page for yourself that incorporates as many page creation capabilities of Composer as you can, without violating good design guidelines. Publish the page if you have access to a Web server.

6 ❱❱❱ The Web site for this book (www.scsite.com/nc/pr3.htm) contains a home page with links to a page for each project. Redesign this site. You may want to reorganize the content and layout of pages, add more pages, reduce the number of pages, change the *look and feel* of the site, or change the way the reader navigates the site.

7 ❱❱❱ Many sources of information on JavaScript are available on the Web. Many of these sites have simple JavaScript functions and routines you can cut and paste into your own pages. Find one of these sources. Cut and paste a JavaScript into any one of the Web pages you already have constructed.

Index

Target(s), adding to template,
  NC 2.41-45
Target image, **NC 2.43-44**
Templates, **NC 2.4**
  adding targets, NC 2.41-45
  categories, NC 2.19
  creating lists, NC 2.37-39
  creating Web pages from,
    NC 2.4-46
  entering and changing text,
    NC 2.24-31
  finding and replacing text,
    NC 2.28-31
  formatting paragraphs in,
    NC 2.34-37
  inserting horizontal lines,
    NC 2.40-41
  linked targets, NC 2.41-45
  local document, NC 2.6
  opening in Composer, NC 2.17-21
  remote document, NC 2.6
  removing links, NC 2.21-24
  setting character properties,
    NC 2.32-34
  testing, NC 2.46
Testing
  local HTML file, NC 1.24-26
  Page Wizard file, NC 1.44
  template, NC 2.46
Text
  alternate, NC 3.18
  copying and pasting from one file
    to another, NC 1.17
  entering and changing in template,
    NC 2.24-31
  finding and replacing in template,
    NC 2.28-31
  links, NC 1.11, NC 3.24
  normal, *see* Normal text
  in table, formatting, NC 3.24-32
  in table, linking to other Web
    pages, NC 3.33-37
  underlined, *see* Underlined text
Text editor
  adding bulleted list, NC 1.19-20
  adding centered heading, NC 1.18
  adding email link, NC 1.20-21
  adding head section, NC 1.17-18
  adding italic text, NC 1.20-21
  adding links to other pages,
    NC 1.19-20

  adding normal text, NC 1.18-19
  adding title, NC 1.17-18
  beginning body, NC 1.18
  centering heading, NC 1.18-19
  creating Web page with,
    NC 1.16-23
Text insertion point, table,
  NC 3.13-14
Texture, **NC 3.9**
3 heading, NC 1.18
Tiled, **NC 1.9**
Tile Vertically command (pop-up
  menu), NC 3.38-39
Title of Web page, **NC 1.9**
  adding using Page Wizard,
    NC 1.29-32
  adding using text editor,
    NC 1.17-18
Title text box (Instructions frame),
  NC 1.30
Toolbars, Composer, NC 2.15-17
TYPE keyword, NC 1.19

Underlined text, clicked to initiate
  link, NC 1.12
Unordered list, **NC 1.19**
URL, of file being linked, NC 1.12
URL text box (Choices frame),
  NC 1.33

Viewing
  document's source, NC 1.12-15
  local HTML file, NC 1.24-26
View menu
  Page Source command,
    NC 1.14-15
View Source command (pop-up
  menu), NC 1.15

Web authoring tools, *see* HTML
  editors
Webmaster, **NC 1.26**
Web page
  background image, NC 3.9-11
  blank, NC 3.7-8
  changing appearance using Page
    Wizard, NC 1.37-40
  copyrighted, NC 2.7
  creating from templates,
    NC 2.4-46

creating using Page Wizard,
  NC 1.7, NC 1.27-44
creating with text editor,
  NC 1.16-23
design guidelines, NC 1.37,
  NC 3.4-5
display in Navigator versus
  Composer windows, NC 1.45
elements, NC 1.8-11
inserting clip art images, NC 3.6-7
inserting tables, NC 3.12-14
linking text and images in table
  to, NC 3.33-37
printing from Composer,
  NC 1.45-46
publishing, NC 1.24, NC 1.26,
  NC 3.48-49
setting properties, NC 3.9-11
signature of, NC 1.37
Web page editors, *see* HTML
  editors
Web page file, transferring to Web
  server, NC 1.24, NC 3.48
Web page templates, *see* Templates
Web server
  copying file to, NC 1.23
  requesting file from, NC 1.6
  transferring Web page file to,
    NC 1.24, NC 3.48
What you see is what you get
  (WYSIWYG), NC 1.27
Width
  cell, NC 3.15
  grid lines surrounding cells,
    NC 1.11
  image, NC 3.41
Window
  browse, *see* Browse window
  Composer, *see* Composer window
  document source, NC 1.15
  Navigator, *see* Navigator window
Word, selecting, NC 2.26
World Wide Web Consortium
  (W3C), **NC 1.8**